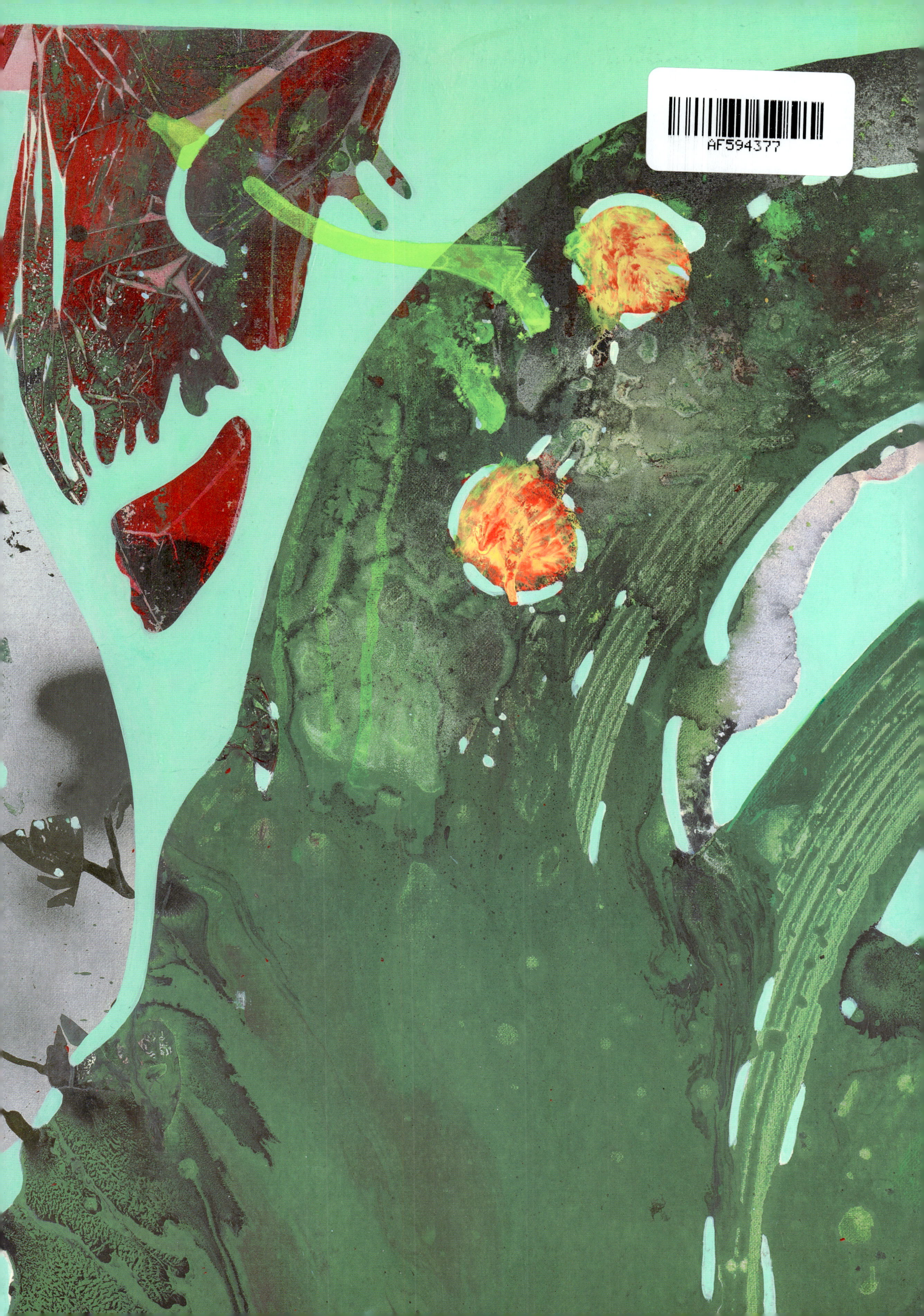
AF594377

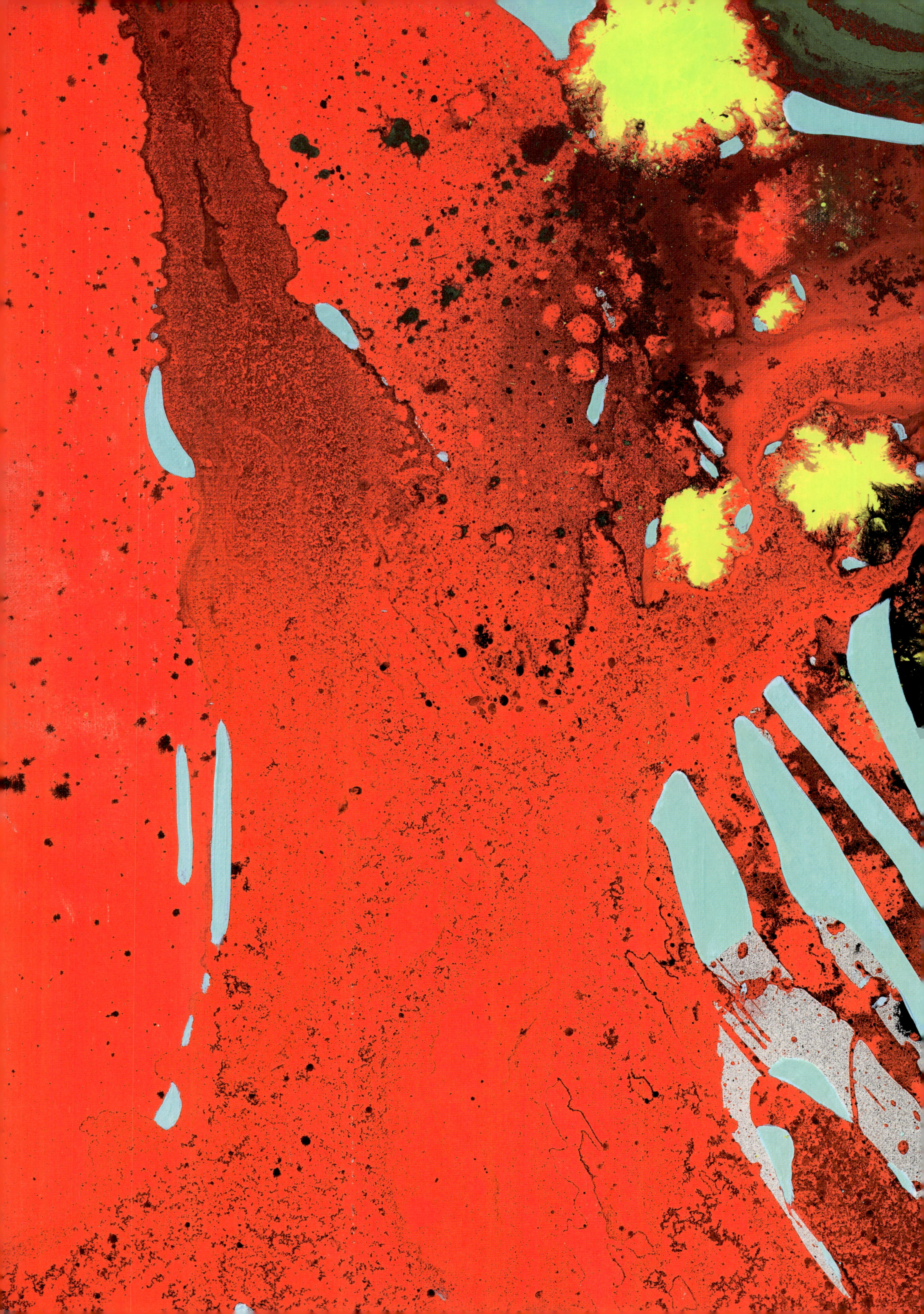

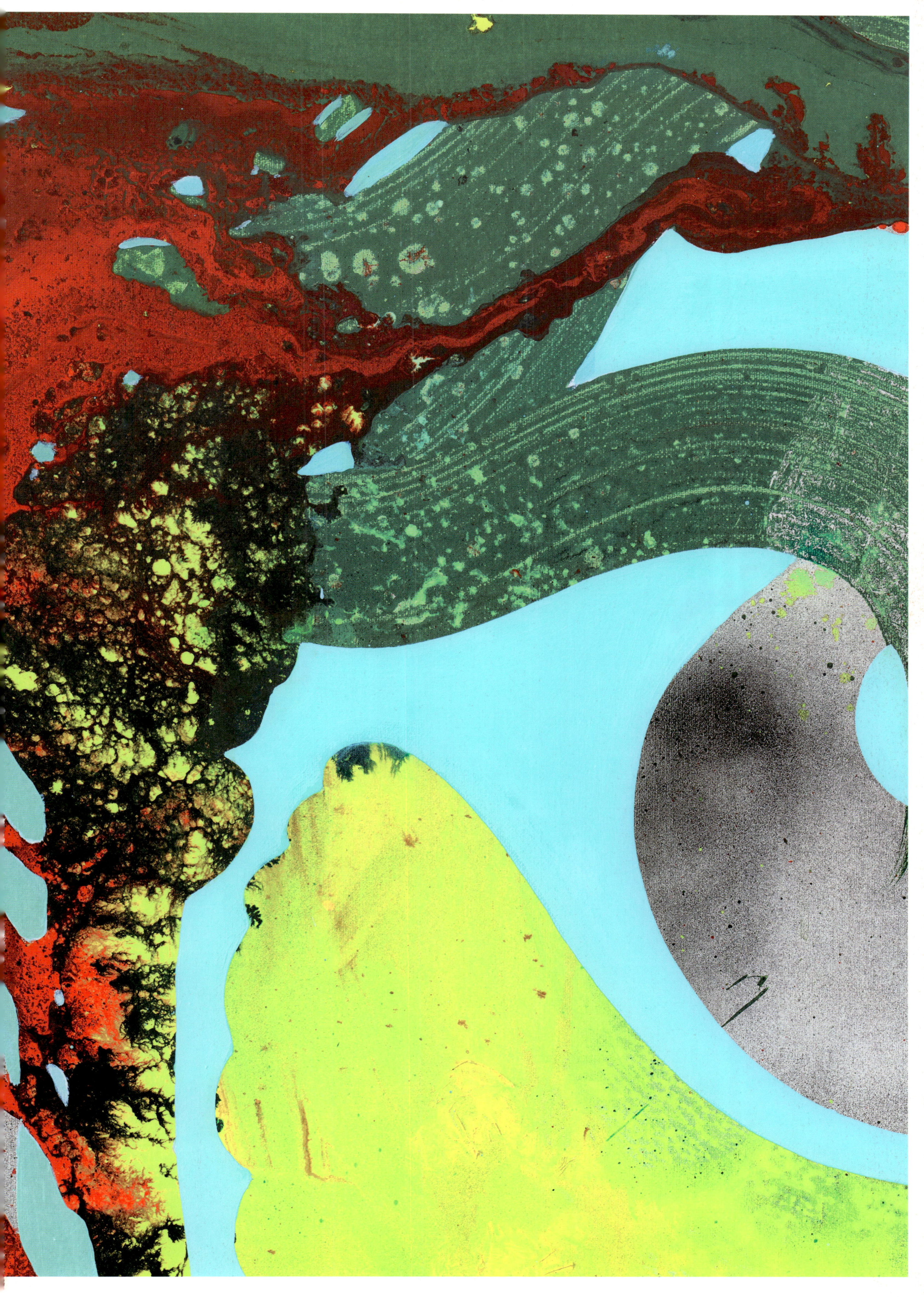

Vian Sora: Outerworlds

Santa Barbara Museum of Art
Speed Art Museum
Asia Society Texas

Edited by Tyler Blackwell and Owen Duffy
Published by Inventory Press

INVENTORY PRESS

Vian Sora

Outerworlds

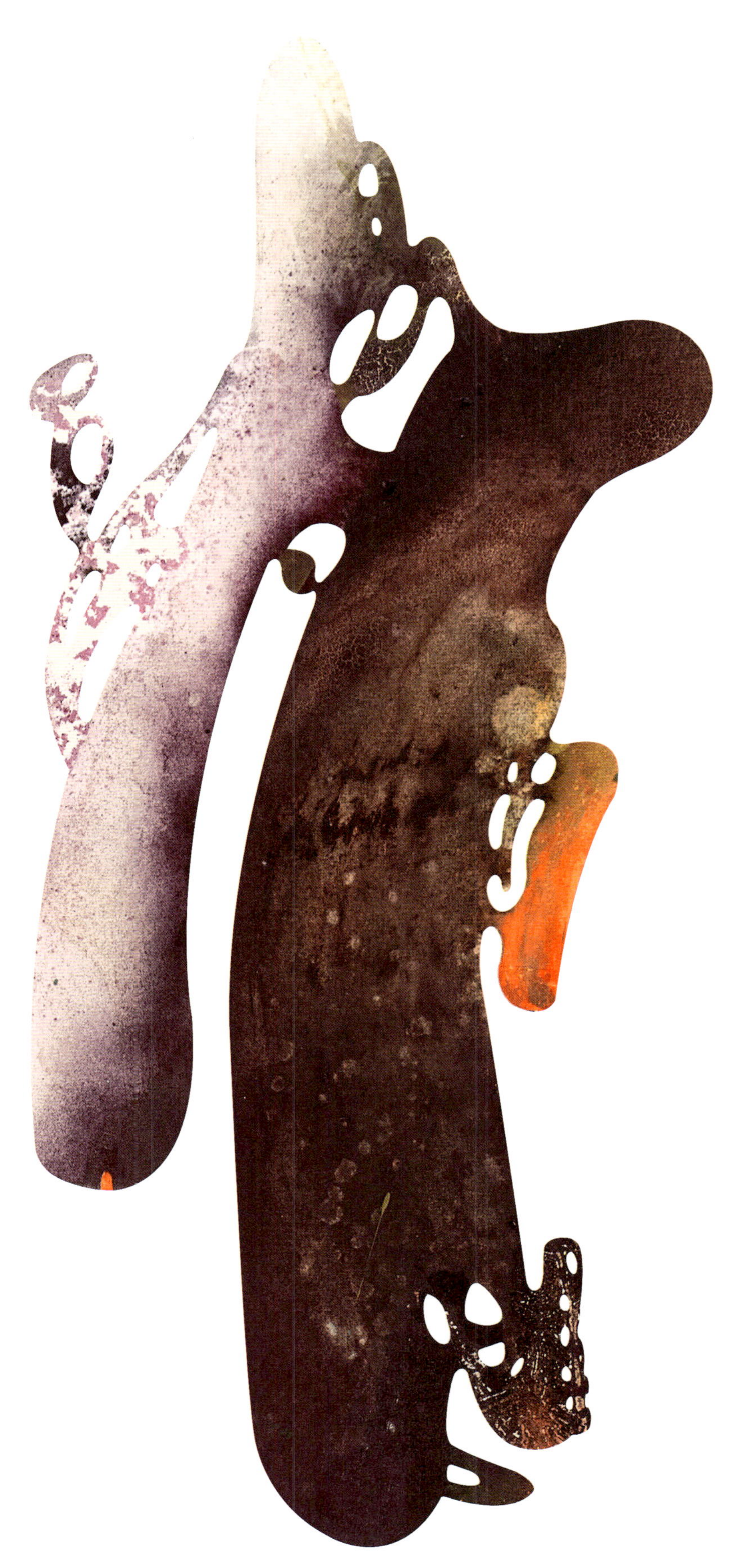

Foreword

Amada Cruz
Bonna Kol
Raphaela Platow

Art is, at its core, a testament to resilience, reinvention, and the boundless human spirit. Few contemporary artists embody these principles as profoundly as Vian Sora. With an artistic voice forged in the crucible of displacement, transformation, and cultural confluence, Sora's work presents a singular vision—one that is both deeply personal and universally resonant. It is with great pride that we present this publication, a comprehensive exploration of her extraordinary career, illuminating the artistic and philosophical depths she has traversed.

Born in Baghdad, a city steeped in the weight of history and the turbulence of modernity, Sora's early experiences were marked by a landscape of contrasts—beauty and destruction, heritage and upheaval. These formative tensions manifest in her work, which pulsates with raw energy, layered narratives, and an aesthetic that defies simple categorization. Drawing from a wide spectrum of influences—ranging from ancient Mesopotamian iconography to European modernism, from Sufi mysticism to contemporary abstraction—Sora creates paintings that are both richly historical and fiercely relevant in today's world.

This volume provides a nuanced examination of her evolving practice, tracing her varied works since 2016, which have borne witness to the psychological and emotional landscapes of war and exile, as well as her unique sublimation of abstraction and daily life, where color, form, and texture become the primary vehicles of expression. Sora's compositions are often turbulent, suffused with urgent, dynamic brushstrokes, embodying a sense of perpetual flux. This reflects not only her own personal migrations—from Iraq to Turkey to the United Arab Emirates to Louisville, Kentucky—but also a broader commentary on displacement, survival, and reinvention.

A particularly compelling aspect of Sora's work is its ability to evoke both personal and collective histories. Her paintings resonate with the echoes of exile, Kurdish diaspora, and the fragmentation of identity—subjects that are increasingly relevant in today's global landscape. Yet rather than dwelling in nostalgia or lament, her work asserts a fierce and unwavering vitality. It is this resilience that defines her practice; her paintings are acts of defiance and affirmation, resisting erasure and insisting on presence.

As institutions dedicated to fostering a dialogue between past and present, tradition and innovation, we recognize in Sora an artist who bridges these divides with remarkable sensitivity and power. Her work challenges conventional narratives of both Southwest Asian and Western art, positioning her as a crucial figure within the international art community. In her hands, paint becomes a conduit for storytelling—stories of resettlement, trauma, rebirth, and above all, the indomitable force of creativity.

This exhibition catalogue serves not only as a record of Sora's remarkable oeuvre but also as a celebration of her enduring contribution to contemporary art. The texts included within these pages, written by leading scholars and curators, offer in-depth analyses of her work, examining its historical references, technical innovations, and thematic complexities. A newly commissioned essay by art historian Suzanne Hudson situates Sora's work within broader art-historical contexts, while an insightful text by Owen Duffy offers a fresh look at the Sora's work within the larger dialogue of America-Middle East relations. Additionally, an illuminating conversation between Tyler Blackwell and Sora provides a deeply personal account of her process, influences, and the ever-shifting terrain of her artistic vision. Together, these contributions provide a richer understanding of Sora's practice, positioning her within both historical traditions and contemporary discourses.

In presenting this publication, we extend our deepest gratitude to Vian Sora for her courage, vision, and unrelenting pursuit of artistic truth. We also acknowledge the many individuals—curators, researchers, collectors, and patrons—who have supported and championed her work over the years. In particular, we thank Tyler Blackwell, Curator of Contemporary Art at the Speed Art Museum, Dr. Owen Duffy, Nancy C. Allen Curator and Director of Exhibitions at Asia Society Texas, and Dr. James Glisson, Chief Curator and Curator of Contemporary Art at the Santa Barbara Museum of Art, for their leadership in bringing this exhibition to life. Their dedication and insight have been invaluable in shaping this project, ensuring that Sora's voice continues to resonate across borders and generations.

For Louisville audiences, this exhibition and catalogue provide an opportunity to celebrate a Kentucky artist whose generosity, vision, and perspective deeply impact fellow artists, friends, and the community. We are immensely grateful to the private lenders who have shared their artworks with us, including Erik Eaker, Judson and Daphne Hartlage, Woo Speed McNaughton, Lopa and Rishabh Mehrotra, Stephanie and Michael Morris, Komal Shah and Gaurav Garg, Brook and Pam Smith, the artist, Drs. Kaveh and Heather Zamanian, and a private collection. We also thank our institutional lenders the Kentucky Performing Arts Foundation, Museum of Contemporary Art San Diego, Santa Barbara Museum of Art, and the Speed Art Museum. This project would not have come to life without the many individuals and organizations whose contributions have been instrumental. In particular, we recognize Julien Robson and the Great Meadows Foundation (along with the late, esteemed Al Shands) for their early encouragement and advocacy. We sincerely appreciate everyone who has helped champion our institutions and Sora's work.

We are also incredibly grateful to Sora's current galleries: Bortolami in New York and The Third Line in Dubai, as well as to David Nolan Gallery, New York; Luis de Jesus, Los Angeles; and Susan Moremen, Louisville. This book is designed beautifully by our partners and friends Max Harvey and Pianpian He, and we are so glad to collaborate with Inventory Press in Los Angeles to co-publish and share this catalogue with friends at home and abroad.

Ultimately, the power of Sora's art lies in its ability to transcend the boundaries of language and geography, speaking instead through the visceral immediacy of color, form, and movement. It is our hope that this monograph serves as an enduring testament to her brilliance and as an invitation for deeper engagement with her ever-evolving artistic journey.

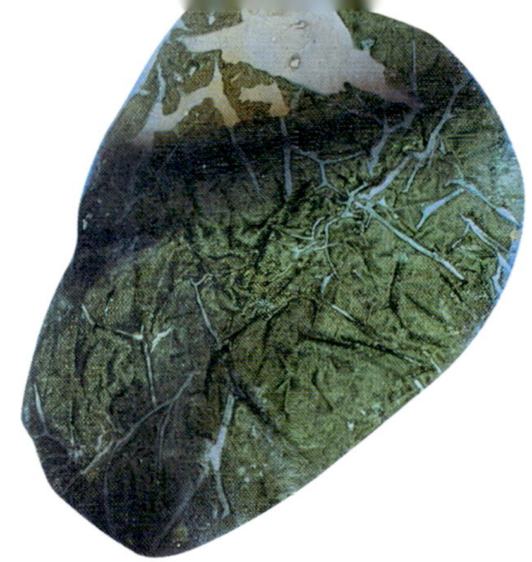

We invite you to explore, reflect, and be moved by the extraordinary world of Vian Sora.

Amada Cruz is the Eichholz Foundation Director of the Santa Barbara Museum of Art.
Bonna Kol is the President of Asia Society Texas.
Raphaela Platow is the former Executive Director of the Speed Art Museum.

Aftershocks of Empire: The Force of Vian Sora's Painting

Owen Duffy

When the dust alights and the paint dries, Vian Sora's works picture explosions in stasis. They are replete with moments of impact, which are paused and seem poised to rewind. Her canvases operate within the fraught territory of memory and materiality, capturing, through pigments powdered and wet, the residue of her lived experience with a striking, powerful immediacy. Born in Baghdad in 1976 to a Kurdish family, much of Sora's life has been characterized by survival, endurance, and the will to create amid dictatorship, invasions, "shock and awe," war, and insurgency. Consequently, a key to Sora's works are their contradictory nature—they are always double-sided or twinned. Destruction and creation ensnare each other. A combustive, and generative, example: *Hanging Gardens* (2022) (plate p. 66). At its heart, the painting contains a central, amorphous form of midnight blues, forest green, and tinges of purple. As if it is rupturing from within, muddy, silty swirls eject outward and reach toward the canvas edge. At the top-left of the composition, follicles of neon-green, flora-like forms sprout into a light blue window. In the space beyond the liquescent bursts, it is difficult to discern what is figure and what is ground, and which color dominates the rest. As in many of Sora's paintings, they are profoundly mesmerizing in their formal dynamism, and the works on view in *Outerworlds*, her first museum retrospective in the United States, emerge after the pivotal year of 2016. During this year, Sora felt that she needed to work with her trauma, the year she realized that she had to deal with what affected her most: explosions.[1] Yet the visual forms also lend themselves to a lusher source, and the painting's title, is, of course, a reference to the Hanging Gardens of ancient Babylon, a crucial hub for various empires in the Mesopotamian region. This series of verdant, tiered gardens—which, like weapons of mass destruction in 2000s Iraq, have not been verified by physical evidence—were purportedly built by the king Nebuchadnezzar II for his wife. And thus, in Sora's paintings, destruction is not an absolute, and is always accompanied by the possibility of growth and becoming.

On the occasion of *Outerworlds*, this essay will propose that Sora's work revels in this fluid space, and not only do the paintings synthesize creation and destruction, but they are at once atavistic and new. They reach into the past for Mesopotamian myth, but they also come to terms with the trauma and tenor of living through twentieth and twenty-first-century Iraq, subject to occupation and insurgency. Sora very much participates in a tradition of modern and contemporary artists using paint and the canvas to picture the boom and the blast, from Pablo Picasso's *Guernica* to Cai-Guo Qiang (b. 1957). Consequently, Sora presents a new vision for this artistic trajectory, colored by the lens of a post-9/11 world, and shaped by awareness of the power of images in the twenty-first century. Sora's works are not only about the thunder of war, however, and there are rich and deep layers to her

1 Interview with the artist, December 13, 2024.

Fig. 1

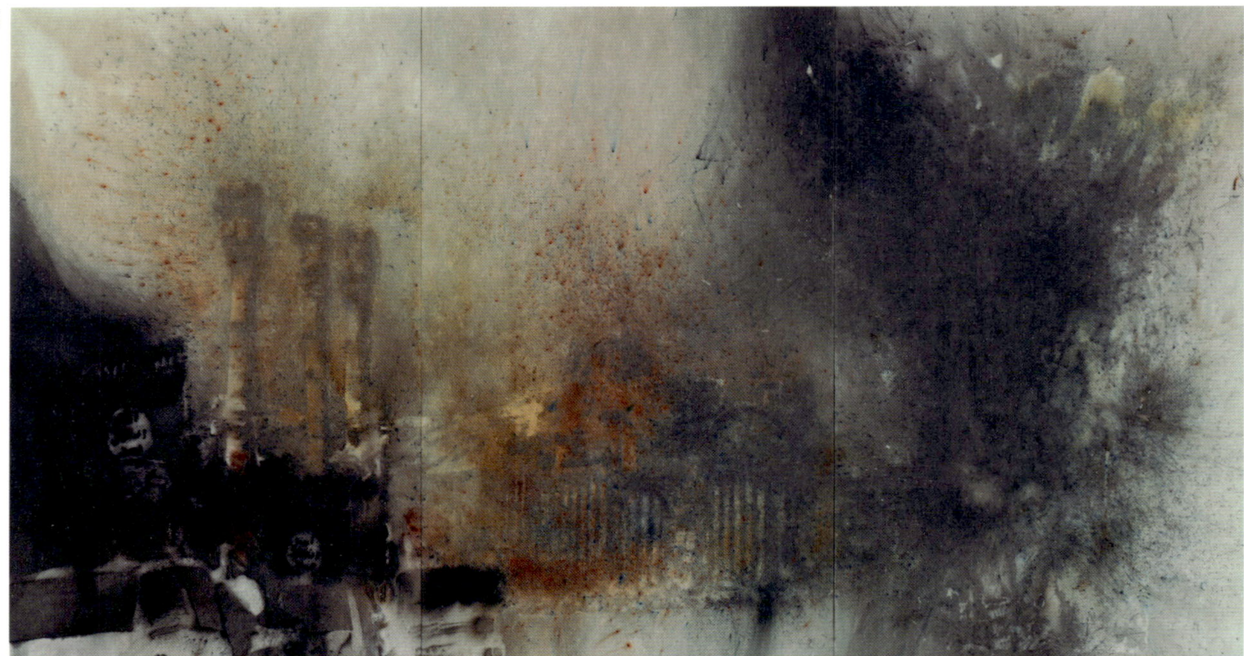

Cai Guo-Qiang, *Palmyra*, 2017. Gunpowder on canvas, 94.5 in. × 177.16 in. (240 cm × 450 cm). Photo by Wen-You Cai; courtesy Cai Studio.

paintings. Her process—defined by working on the floor of her studio with canvas, which becomes a repository of pours and spills—builds on the legacy of many groundbreaking abstract painters, notably Helen Frankenthaler (1928–2011). This essay will contextualize the notion of the pour, the spill, and the stain in relationship to Sora's predecessors, and propose its renewed significance today.

Sora participates in a tradition of painting as a means of representing the ineffable violence of war, but, more specifically, of artists working with explosions, their force, and their aftermath. Relevant to Sora's sociohistorical context, Picasso's *Guernica* (1937), currently in the collection of Museo Reina Sofia in Madrid, but reproduced as a tapestry hung in the United Nations Security Council chamber, emerges as an undeniable correlation. The greyscale work depicts the horrors of Nazi Germany and Fascist Italy raining bombs on a Basque town. In 2003, the UN infamously curtained off the tapestry for Colin Powell and John Negroponte as they attempted to argue for military intervention in Iraq. The American government attempted to control this powerful image, concerned about the optics of advocating for invasion against an anti-war backdrop. Decades later, the painting's absence, and the irony of the moment, is still remembered. There's also Yves Klein, known for his intensely saturated canvases blanketed with his signature blue, who worked with France's national gas company to produce a series of paintings torched with a flamethrower in 1961. Michael Heizer (b. 1944) dynamited two sides of a Nevada mesa to make his landmark earthwork *Double Negative* (1969). More recently, Cai Guo-Qiang has achieved recognition for detonating gunpowder onto canvases into quasi-controlled patterns (fig. 1). Working with this technique for almost forty years, Cai deploys gunpowder as a fecund material weighted in the history and traditions of China, who, like Sora, finds union in the language of creation and destruction. Sora, however, departs from the literalness and heavy-handedness of some of her predecessors, who use the explosion to move tons of earth or to offer spectacle. Instead, Sora uses paint to poetically remake the sense of force that accompanies detonation, which becomes a structuring agent for the painted image, a conceptual crater into which she pours history, memory, and myth. Moreover, Sora has *lived through* the forcefulness suggested by her works; which differentiates her from distanced observers or *expérimentateurs*. Working for the Associated Press from 2003 to 2006, she accompanied journalists to cover the grim effects of bombing and insurgency. "I was covering explosion scenes immediately after they happened, taking news crews there," she reflects, "I witnessed things no one should witness."[2]

2 Vian Sora, quoted in Katie White, "Iraqi-American Artist Vian Sora Evokes the Splendor of Eden and Ancient Assyria in Her Paintings," *Artnet News*, November 21, 2023, https://news.artnet.com/art-world/vian-sora-david-nolan-2395358.

Fig. 2

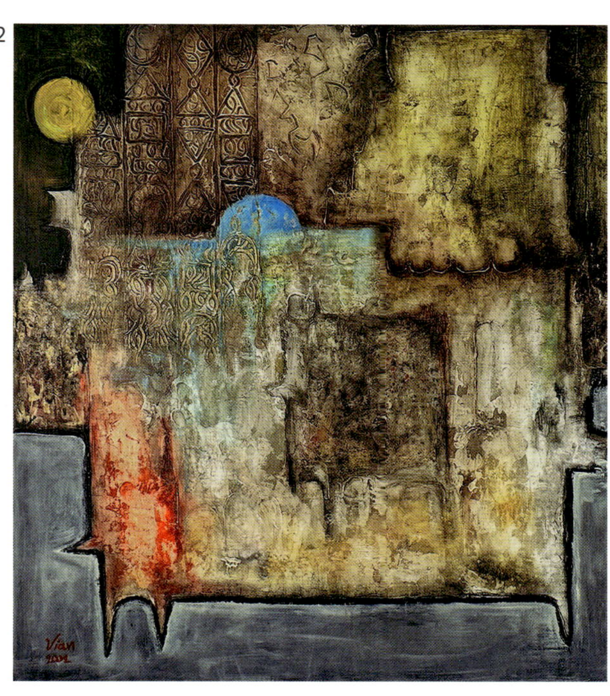

Vian Sora, *Pray*, 2001. Oil on canvas, 46 in. × 46 in. (117 cm × 117 cm). Courtesy the artist.

The most powerful, world-shaping image of an explosion in recent history is undoubtedly the one produced on the morning of September 11, 2001, when hijackers flew planes into the World Trade Center towers in New York City. Sora's work, which grapples with the reality of war-ripped Iraq, engages—through a particular lens—with the fallout of this image's production and circulation. Watching this image dominate media networks from her home in Baghdad, Sora was profoundly impacted, and this chain of events ultimately led to her emigration from Iraq. "Around the time of my first solo show at an art gallery in Baghdad," Sora recalls, after watching the towers fall on television, she felt that "my world is going to change ... something is going to happen in our country that is related to this event."[3]

One of the most compelling interpretations of 9/11—and one that sheds light on the function of Sora's paintings—can be found in *Afflicted Powers: Capital and Spectacle in the New Age of War* (2005), written by the anti-imperial collective Retort. This text, marked by its accessible, broadside-like tone, presents a thesis on how images operate in geopolitics: as active agents, fired like projectiles that explode into cultural and political shrapnel. Retort's manifesto for the early 2000s examines the events of September 11, the invasion of Iraq, and the rise of political Islam, all within 217 pages. Their book was written as millions of people around the world gathered to protest the impending invasion of Iraq—an event that would also irreparably alter Sora's life, along with countless others. Retort's central argument posits that we exist at a liquid historical juncture that is simultaneously hypermodern and brutally atavistic. Barbaric ideologies, like those held by the 9/11 hijackers, seek to enact violence and retribution to generate the very images that dominate our current cultural condition. "A picture, in the present condition of politics," counsels Retort, "is itself, if sufficiently well executed, a specific and effective piece of statecraft."[4] Thus, September 11 "happened" as an actual event only insofar as it etched into the collective memory of the United States a terrifying and potent image of empire's collapse—hijacking not only aircraft but the global media itself. According to Retort, "the horrors of September 11 were designed above all to be visible."[5]

The production—and destruction—of images has become an undeniably integral component of statecraft, and only more so since the beginning of this century. In the years following September 11, the United States waged endless war as part of a larger "struggle for mastery in the realm of the image," as Retort's protagonists propose.[6] Remarkably

3 Interview with the artist, January 9, 2025. All subsequent quotes regarding *Pray* come from this interview.

4 Retort, *Afflicted Powers: Capital and Spectacle in the New Age of War* (Verso, 2005), 26.

5 Ibid.

6 Retort, *Afflicted Powers*, 19.

Fig. 3

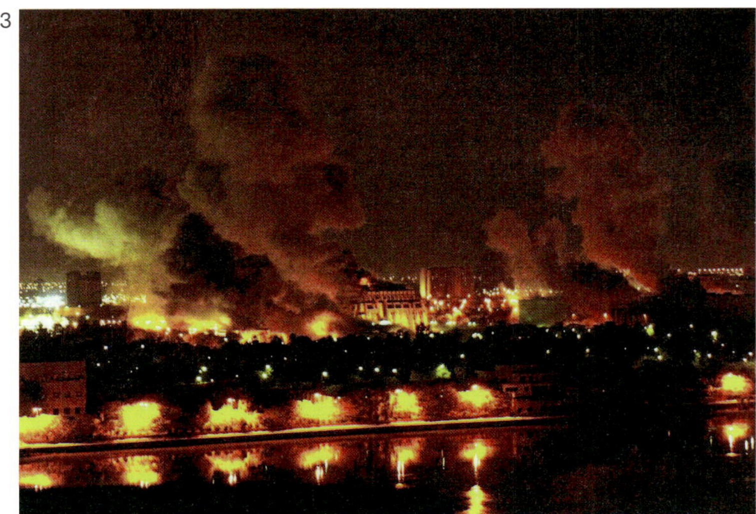

Baghdad during the American-led "shock and awe" campaign. Courtesy Daily Mirror Gulf coverage.

prescient, one can extrapolate from the lessons of *Afflicted Powers* and bring newfound understanding to so many events since September 11. The campaign of "shock and awe" endeavored to supplant the picture of September 11, punctuated with a weak-tea visual to convince spectators "mission accomplished." Bearing this in mind, those who produce and interpret images should not be surprised, then, when the militants of the Islamic State released iconoclastic videos, sledgehammering Assyrian statues or their plaster replicas. These videos exist as forms of weaponized image-making that succinctly capture the anachronic double-bind of heartless old-fashionedness and contemporary conduits of media distribution. In the twenty-first century, conflict resides in the realm of the image, and what is at stake is the very picture of world.

Through her work, Sora intuitively interprets the new role of images in the twenty-first century, and has operated in this space since September 11. That evening in Baghdad, Sora responded to this singular act of terrorism, which she knew would alter her life, as well. She responded by painting *Pray* (2001; fig. 2), which she described, ominously, as "a prediction of what happened later."[7] At the painting's center, a half-dome of turquoise rests above an abstracted edifice. This silhouetted structure is surrounded by competing, shifting planes of gold, copper, and green, and the style echoes the work of such Iraqi modernists as Kahdim Hayder (1932–1985). The edges of the various planes blur, dissolve, and flicker in flames of paint, and a yellow disc hovers in the top left corner of the canvas. Sora carved swirling characters, a hybridized calligraphic script that references Arabic and cuneiform, and the cumulative result is a composition that captures on one hand a sense of hope that the events of September 11 will not result in war, but also models "what our cities will look like after devastation." When compared with a 2003 image of Baghdad (fig. 3)—its skyline filled with choking black smoke and flames—captured by Sora's friend Hamza Abas from her Associated Press office, where she worked as a journalist, the work becomes strikingly prescient. It anticipates the "shock and awe" military strategy of spectacular force that the United States deployed as a counter-image to the wound of 9/11. Sora herself made a painting after 2003 titled *Shock and Awe*, which she later exhibited and sold in Turkey. However, after moving multiple times and eventually fleeing Iraq due to her journalism, which led to death threats from insurgents, Sora did not retain documentation of the work. Throughout this historical period, Sora remained keenly aware of the power of images, and the salvos of destruction required to produce them.

7 As an individual work of art, *Pray* anticipated the next decade of Sora's life. Not only the devastation of Iraq, but her now husband, Jed Hayden, actually purchased paintings prior to meeting Sora. They would subsequently meet in London in 2005.

Fig. 4

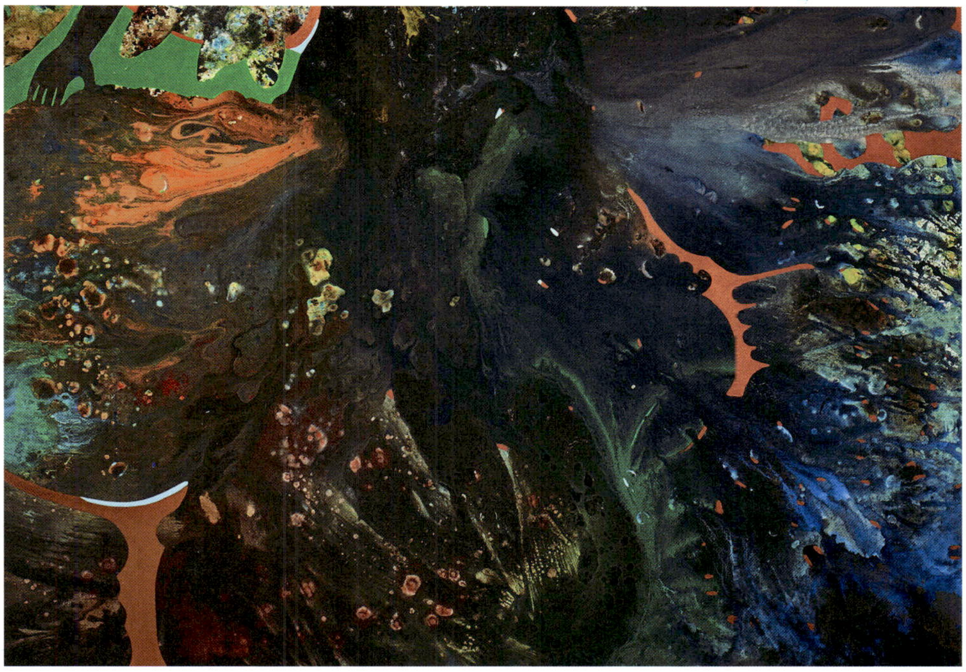

Vian Sora, detail of *Abzu*, 2023. Oil, acrylic, and pigment on canvas, 84 in. × 350 in. (2.13 m × 8.89 m). Photo by Chad Crews; courtesy the artist.

In more recent works, Sora builds on the groundwork of *Pray*—the beginning of a renewed cycle of violence the painting seemed to anticipate—to present explosive visions of paint. Through these works, Sora shows viewers the instability of and the power within images. Paintings like *Abzu* (2023; plate p. 48) are also iconoclastic in nature, and present this challenging duality of the old and the new in a monumental scale. For Sora, *Abzu* represents a massive outpouring of emotions, and the scale signals an achievement in terms of painted physicality. It was created over the course of three months, and by design, the painting emerged across five panels, hinting at bodies in flux surrounded by fire, water, landslides, and verdant fields. In describing her creative process, Sora explains, "I initiate each of my works with the canvas flat, then I utilize fast-drying spray paint, acrylics, pigments and inks, applying each ... with brushes, sponges, spray bottles or my breath to move the medium, creating passages ... like ventricles, sometimes tissue."[8] The result is a highly saturated ground upon which she builds a reverse archaeology of paint, adding layer after layer like the accretion of geological sediment. "I then use oil to control the disarray, layering various hues in an intuitive process," says Sora, functioning as an attempt "to constrain chaos, when life regenerates from detritus."[9] *Abzu* is an example of this process *par excellence* (fig. 4).

The title of the painting references the Sumerian term for the fresh water from underground aquifers that helped fertilize the region. For ancient Sumerians, the word was infused with cosmological dimensions, and conjured the idea of a freshwater ocean, both above and below the earth, creating the possibility of agriculture, and life.[10] In Sora's monumental painting, aquamarines spill, or flood, outward from the center of each panel. Moments of fire—passages of vivid, flaming tangerine paint—burst intermittently. In the panel second from the left, the full cycle of color and form manifest, from the verdant upgrowths to the lateral slip of earth. It is as, according to Santa Barbara Museum of Art Chief Curator James Glisson, "if there was an entire world laid down on the canvas."[11] There are moments of fire and water coming together, as well as moments of harmony. For Sora, this painting represents the cyclical nature of history, and allows her to emphasize her heritage, as it is such an important part of her life, being half Arab, but identifying as Kurdish.

8 Vian Sora, quoted in Christa Terry, "Art as Resistance: Vian Sora on Veiled Meaning and Unleashed Expression," *Observer*, May 14, 2024, https://observer.com/2024/05/interview-artist-vian-sora-independent-new-york/

9 Ibid.

10 While integral to the cosmology of ancient Mesopotamian peoples, Abzu also references a deity, made of fresh water, from the Babylonian creation epic, *Enuma Elish*.

11 James Glisson, quoted in the Speed Art Museum press release for *Vian Sora: Outerworlds*, January 15, 2025. Published by the Speed Art Museum.

Fig. 5

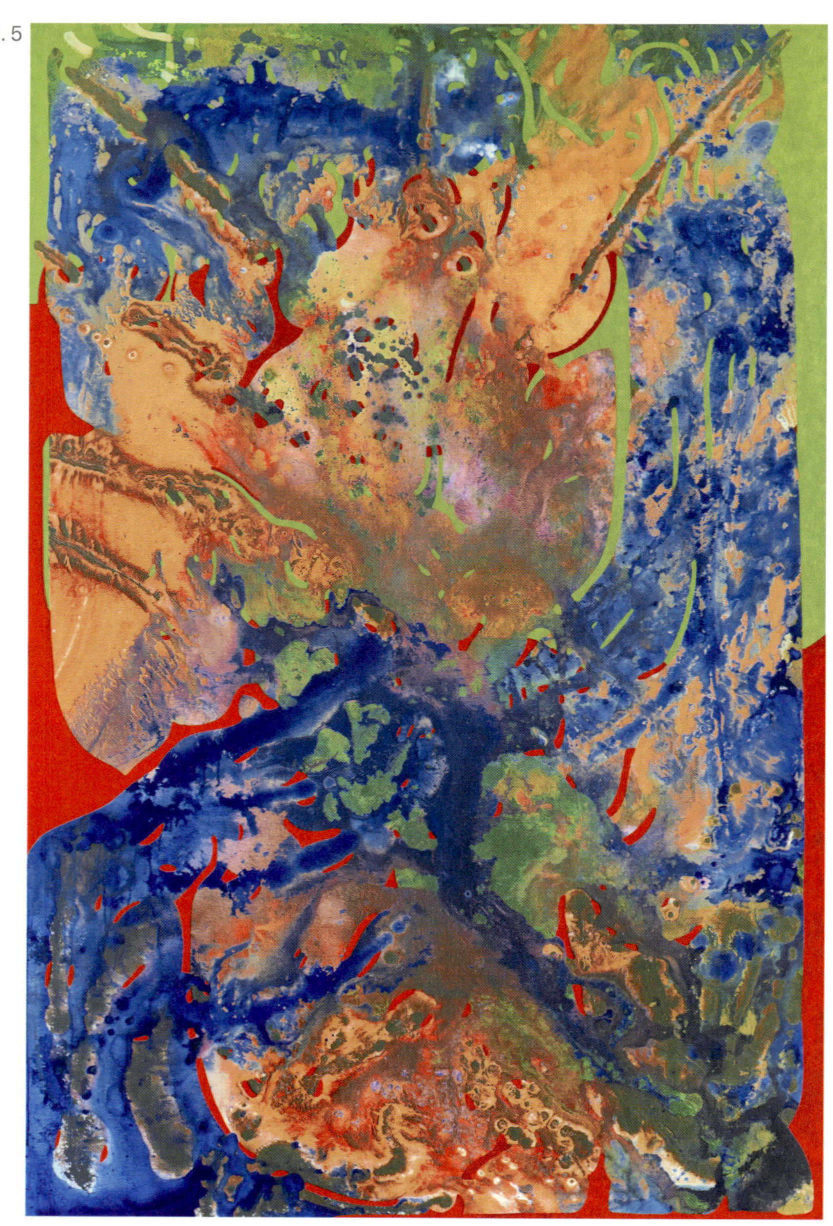

Vian Sora, *Noosphere*, 2024. Oil, acrylic, and pigment on canvas, 72 in. × 48 in. (183 cm × 122 cm). Photo by Chad Crews; courtesy the artist.

But Sora does not merely represent explosions through her work as a means of processing trauma. In the exercise of making these works Sora articulates the flows—of information, of people, of conflicts—that make the networked world of the twenty-first century so dynamic and volatile. Yet, through the process of painting Sora flattens what is normally three-dimensional within the subjugated space of the picture plane. Indeed it is a means through which Sora can exercise a sense of pictorial agency over the three-dimensional nature of the shockwaves and explosions. Shock and awe is reigned in, reignited, and manipulated through form.

More recently, Sora's newer pieces, such as *Noosphere* (2024; fig. 5)—beyond the scope of this exhibition—extend her signature tension by merging conflicting perspectives, yet they introduce a sense of optimism while retaining the mesmerizing chaos of her earlier oeuvre. These works challenge perception with their inverted creation: painted horizontally on the studio floor, they are later elevated to meet the standing viewer's gaze. This confrontation generates a spatial dynamic that resists illusion, instead evoking an aerial perspective—a view from above, as if from a plane, the vehicle that unites the globe yet doubles as the harbinger of bombing. The result is disorienting, a vertiginous experience of land and history, layered like an archaeological dig. Sora's compositions reference many elements, from landscape and biology to the history of modernist painting, and her technique—working from above and saturating the canvas—invites comparison to Helen Frankenthaler. The Manhattan-born Abstract Expressionist, pioneer of the "soak-stain" method, similarly worked on canvases laid flat on the floor. Emerging in the 1950s and '60s, Frankenthaler was championed by critic Clement Greenberg, who featured her in his landmark exhibition

Fig. 6

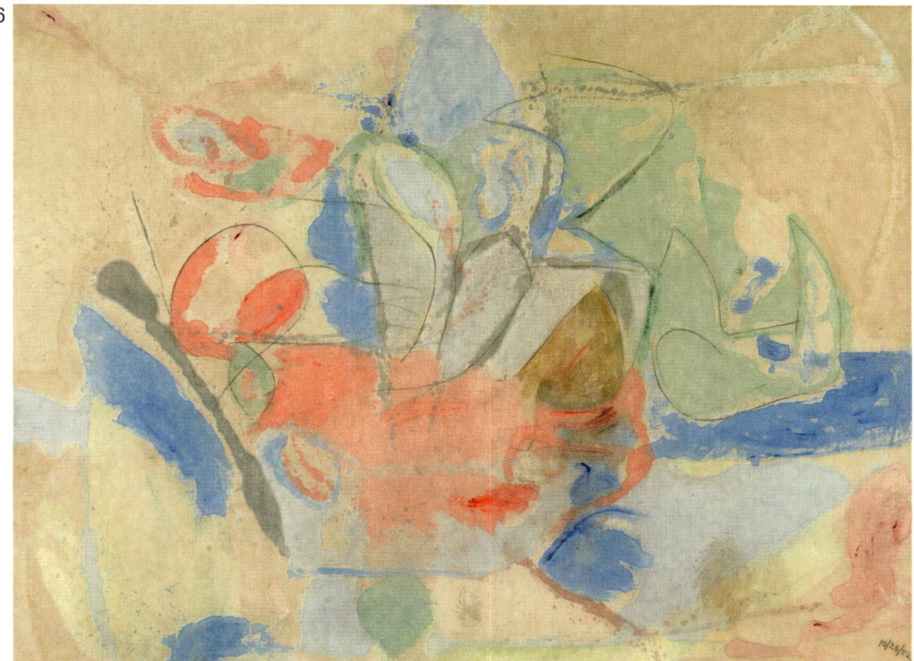

Helen Frankenthaler, *Mountains and Sea*, 1952. Oil and charcoal on unsized, unprimed canvas, 86 ⅜ × 117 ¼ inches (219.4 × 297.8 cm).

Post-Painterly Abstraction at Los Angeles County Museum of Art (LACMA) in 1964. Her 1952 breakthrough, *Mountains and Sea* (fig. 6), created at the age of twenty-three after a visit to coastal Nova Scotia, epitomizes her approach. The painting, with its seafoam greens, baby blues, and rosy pinks framed by darker, linear forms, achieves an ethereal quality through her method of pouring thinned oil paint directly onto unprimed linen. The stains represent, from a formalist perspective, a supreme union between paint and substrate, a defining feature of midcentury abstraction, but also have been unfairly gendered by art critics, and coded to reference bodily functions, such as menstruation.[12] *Mountains and Sea* is a magisterial composition, a soothing yet erratic landscape that feels perpetually in flux—finished yet teeming with potential, asking where a painting begins and ends.

While their processes intertwine in notable ways, the socio-historical contexts shaping Sora's paintings stand in stark contrast to those of Frankenthaler, who was raised amid the affluence of Upper East Side Manhattan and came of age as an artist during the postwar economic boom. This disparity underscores a peculiar irony: the expansiveness of Frankenthaler's groundbreaking canvases evokes the ease and optimism of a burgeoning America, buoyed by its economic ascendancy. As hallmarks of Abstract Expressionism, her paintings seamlessly aligned with Cold War cultural diplomacy, serving as emblems of freedom in service of American foreign policy. Recently, critics have revisited the alignments between Abstract Expressionism, America's cultural intelligentsia, and the State Department during the Cold War.[13] In this century, Sora's work is staking out new terrain. Vian Sora's paintings differ from Frankenthaler's in their emphasis on narrative and personal history, as Sora often explores themes of displacement, resilience, and socio-political upheaval, moving beyond a focus on abstraction for its own sake. Ultimately, Sora's works are grounded in contemporary tensions and personal experience, contrasting with Frankenthaler's pursuit of timeless, meditative abstraction. Crucially, Sora's abstraction interrogates the human and cultural costs of failed statecraft and interventionist geopolitics, reframing the genre of painting as a space to reckon with the aftershocks of empire.

12 For more information on the gendered discourse surrounding Helen Frankenthaler's work, please see Lisa Saltzman, "Reconsidering the Stain: On Gender and the Body in Helen Frankenthaler's Painting," in Norma Broude and Mary D. Garrard (eds.), *Reclaiming Female Agency: Feminist Art History After Postmodernism* (University of California Press, 2005).

13 See Lucy Levine, "Was Modern Art Really a CIA Psy-Op?" in JSTOR Daily, April 1, 2020, https://daily.jstor.org/was-modern-art-really-a-cia-psy-op/.

Vian Sora: Floodgates

Suzanne Hudson

In 2021, Vian Sora held a solo exhibition at Moremen Gallery, in her adopted hometown of Louisville, Kentucky. She called it *Floodgates*, the name belonging to the eponymous painting (2021; plate p. 40), and a group of recent mixed-media paintings collected under its sign. The Oxford English Dictionary parses the noun, in the singular, as a gate that "may be opened or closed, to admit or exclude water," a sluice for excessive surges. But the secondary definition registers a torrent of another kind, "relating to rain or tears." Physical and figurative, it might describe an outpouring, a response to trauma that is environmental or bodily, collective or individual. In this it accrues particular significance in the context of the COVID-19 pandemic during which she made this series, though Sora's invocations of water—moving more than static—are ubiquitous. As befits her Heraclitean embrace of flux, meanings shift according both to specific references that Sora introduces (e.g., Abzu, the Sumerian term for fresh water pooled in underground aquifers, that graces a truly epic painting extending across five panels, *Abzu* (2023; plate p. 48); the Old Testament deluge of Noah; Enki, a Sumerian god of water; and so on) and interpretive milieus beyond her.

Born in Baghdad, Sora's titles invoke millennia of Iraq's textual and material history. (Take, for instance, *Hanging Garden* (2022; plate p. 66), pointing to the Mesopotamian Hanging Gardens of Babylon; one of the seven wonders of the ancient world, it was supposedly built by Nebuchadnezzar as a gift to his wife Semiramis, a Persian princess, to ease her homesickness.) These citations likewise lead up to the much nearer past. Sora's Kurdish family was subject to surveillance and persecution under Saddam Hussein. They experienced at close range the brutalities of the Iran-Iraq War (1980–88), the Gulf War (1991), and the invasion of Iraq by America and its allies in 2003. Detonations that she witnessed as a civilian and while working for the Associated Press in the early 2000s have animated Sora's compositions; and since 2016, Sora has reversed explosion scenes to instead reveal something of the lushness of life. Still, many paintings further suggest the border fetish of ethno-national geopolitics as topographical maps or aerial views of landscapes at a distance, as though seen from a plane. Her signature forms—striated and physically altered by contact, bursting and seeping beyond themselves as figures against equally unstable grounds—likewise suggest in their palettes of burning phosphorescence conflict's perpetual aftermath as chemical and ecological consequence.

In their plays of parts, these paintings model dissolution and reconstitution. Sora builds them from the ground up, with layers creating meaning in their overlap and disambiguation. The results as images are undecidedly terrestrial or biomorphic, often harboring content that feels both tangible and out of reach. Sora does start with a figure, rendering a contour in marks drawn fast with charcoal. This mediates what comes next, even if the presence of such embodied calligraphy is only residual. Sora describes this tendency to cloak the subject as a strategic method, one that began from necessity that it outlives: painting in Baghdad, as a woman, ever aware of the stakes of visibility, there was an impetus to veil iconography and association. Now taking hold of the support and its narrative cipher, Sora turns it flat; once horizontal, Sora uses high flow acrylics, spray paint, and others, adding and stripping passages that coat but also preserve the tension of the surface. Settling the backdrop, as boundaries between aspects emerge, she uses them to instantiate and then reciprocally determine structure, and against which to exert control. Through freehand brushwork, absent stencils or other implements, she might paint some forty to sixty layers, effectively sculpting liquid into coruscating nebulae that also remain very obviously paint—with oil paint as the tool employed to order the generative chaos.

In leaving her process so clearly observable, Sora effectively thematizes it as a kind of means and end, analogizing studio work to other modes of changeability. ***Morphing*** (2023; plate p. 69), is especially clear on Sora's twinning of painterly and subjective becoming. It looks to be in a state of arrested motion, and in its golds and metallics, perhaps on its way to verdigris in concept if not chemistry. Color is evidently settling into unrepeatable arrangements, left in a state that admits an acceptance of the provisional. Set against a tripartite backing—large monochromatic swathes of goldenrod, turquoise, and cerulean—the visible action of morphing holds the center, as petal-like segments radiate from its recesses. This painting is forthright about its self-reflexive posture, its grappling with what it means to change from within but always necessarily exist, and grow, in relation. Sora insists on the connection of all works to her lived experience, even as her refusal of fixity in method as well as meaning allows for others—for the outer world—to find very different resonances within the same shapes. If anything, her work seems to solicit positionalities of viewing that do not align or might even prove irresoluble.

Put another way, Sora's work crucially contends that the forms carry meaning within and in excess of themselves—meaning that she might intend but never presumes to control. In this openness to the receiver, she refuses the self-sufficiency claimed by modernist abstraction, or at least its most prominent critical interlocutors, including Clement Greenberg. The child of an art gallery owner and antiques dealer, Sora has long looked at art and read about it voraciously, consuming often incommensurable histories of art of West Asia, Europe, and North America that frame her contemporary interventions into these extant discourses. As relates to her technique, the example of second-generation Abstract Expressionism is a touchstone, albeit one that Sora actively reformulates. Material contingency born of pouring or staining, sloshing and mixing, is now synonymous with Helen Frankenthaler's paintings of the 1950s. Adopting Jackson Pollock's drip painting to a pour, Frankenthaler allowed transparent colors to bleed into unprimed supports as she worked on the floor; there, they self-arranged through an aleatory orchestration that transpired within the limits that she had imposed from the start. Frankenthaler reasserted authorship differently when she hung the painting back on the wall and found in its patterns something recognizable (if not predetermined or worked for deliberately with an objective correlative as in naturalistic representation).

As introduced above, for her part Sora acknowledges that "[b]odies are always there, deep under the colors." Because she lays down the figures before the washes and oil layers, her would-be abstraction is never "pure," or in modernist-speak, autonomous. That the figure might be a sort of self-portraiture, a surrogate for Sora in the painting, or that it might belong to her only insofar as she is its maker and first viewer, is something that Sora leaves ambiguous. She will acknowledge the apposition of *Landscape with a Moth* (2016; plate p. 54), to a period of rebirth born of surgery and bodily fragility, and moreover offer that this time proved a crucible that changed her and her painting irrevocably. The issue as understood through Sora's work, then, is perhaps less that Abstract Expressionism was or was not autonomous, but rather that male critics took it to be—or demanded that it should be—cleaved from external reference. Sora's radical vulnerability, and the position of strength that she finds in it, invites one to glean "content" in her work. By extension, it helps one to imagine how it was always there. To open the floodgates is to enact a corrective or revisionist feminist history. It is also a manifesto for the present.

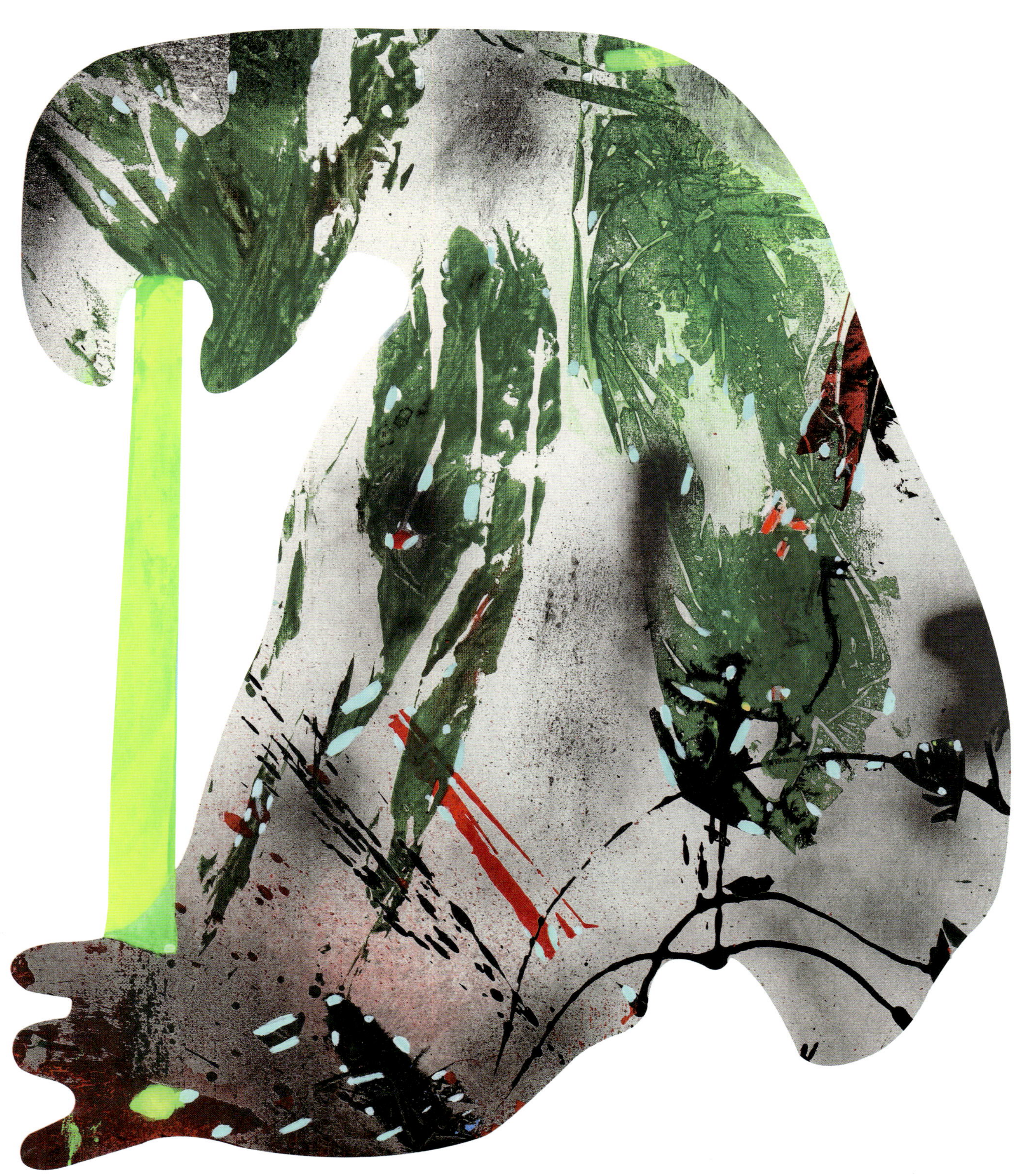

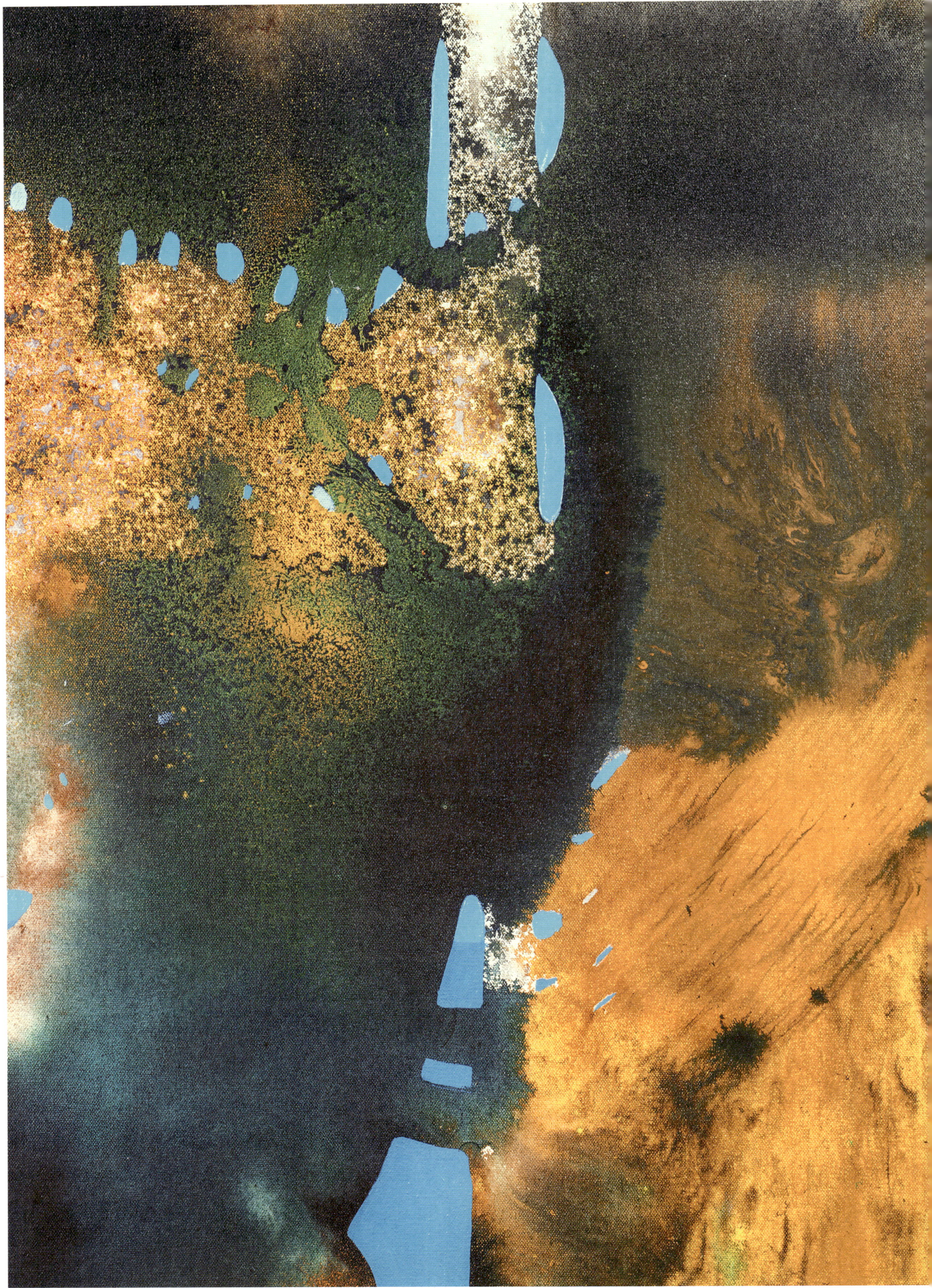

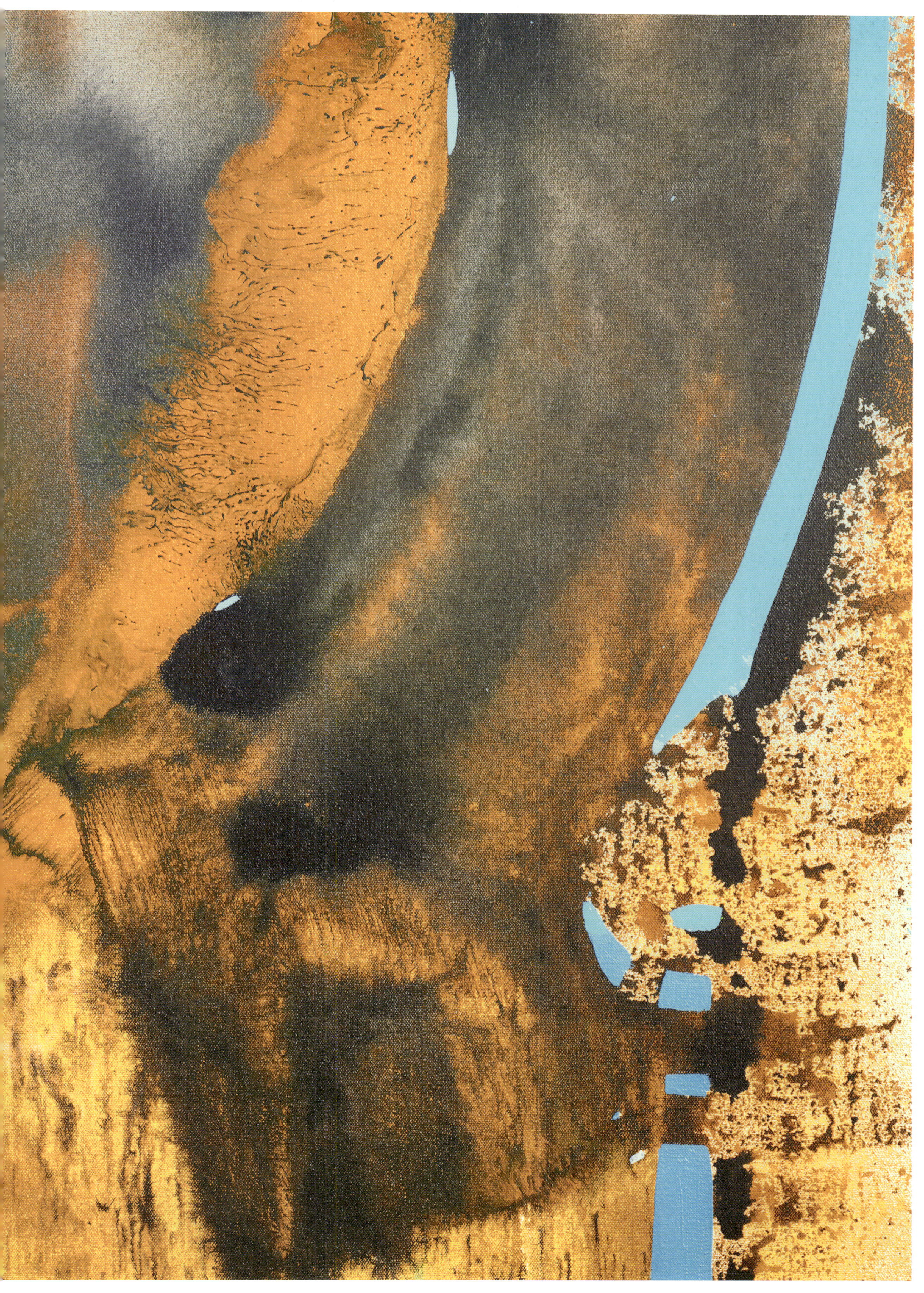

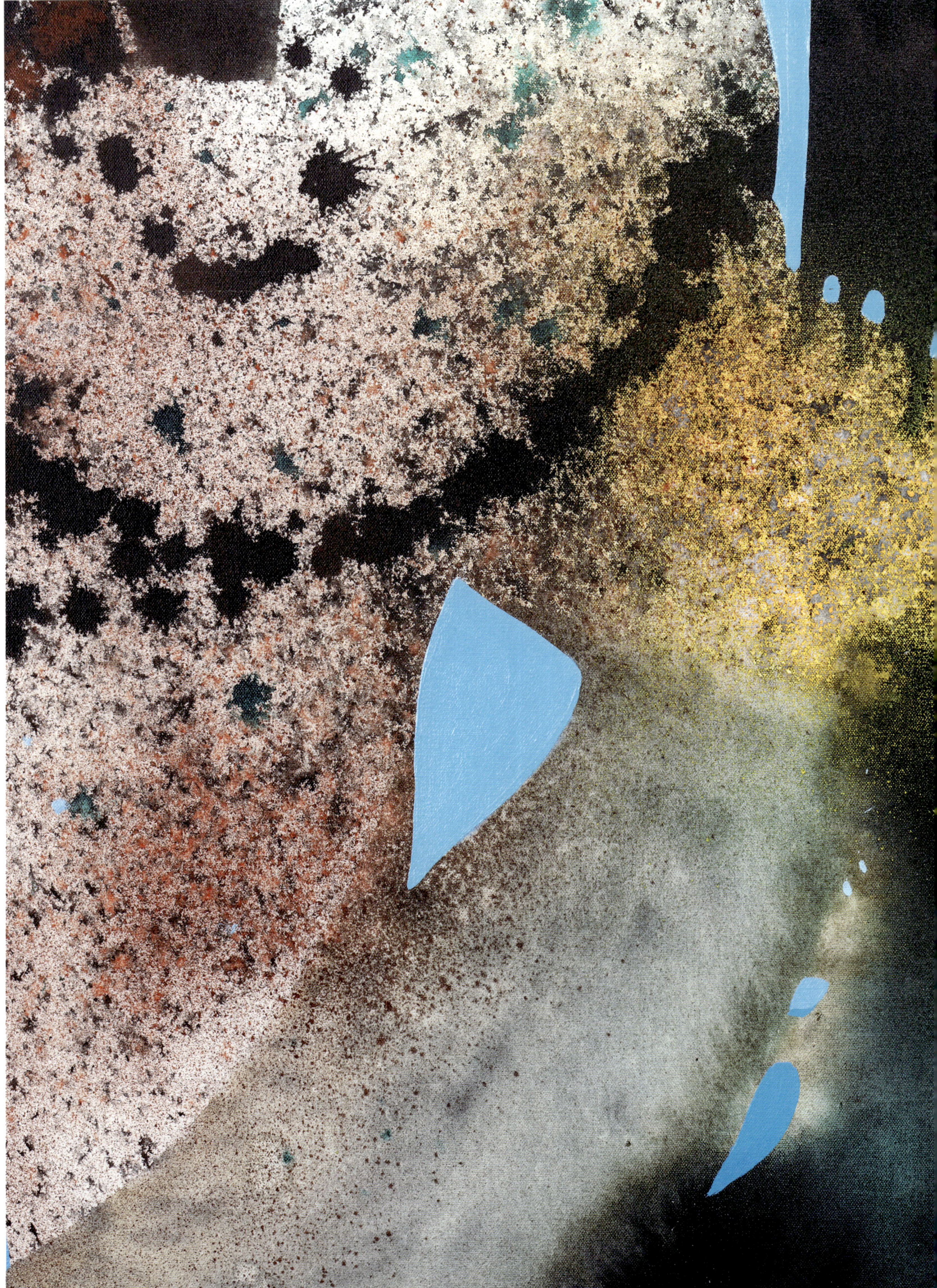

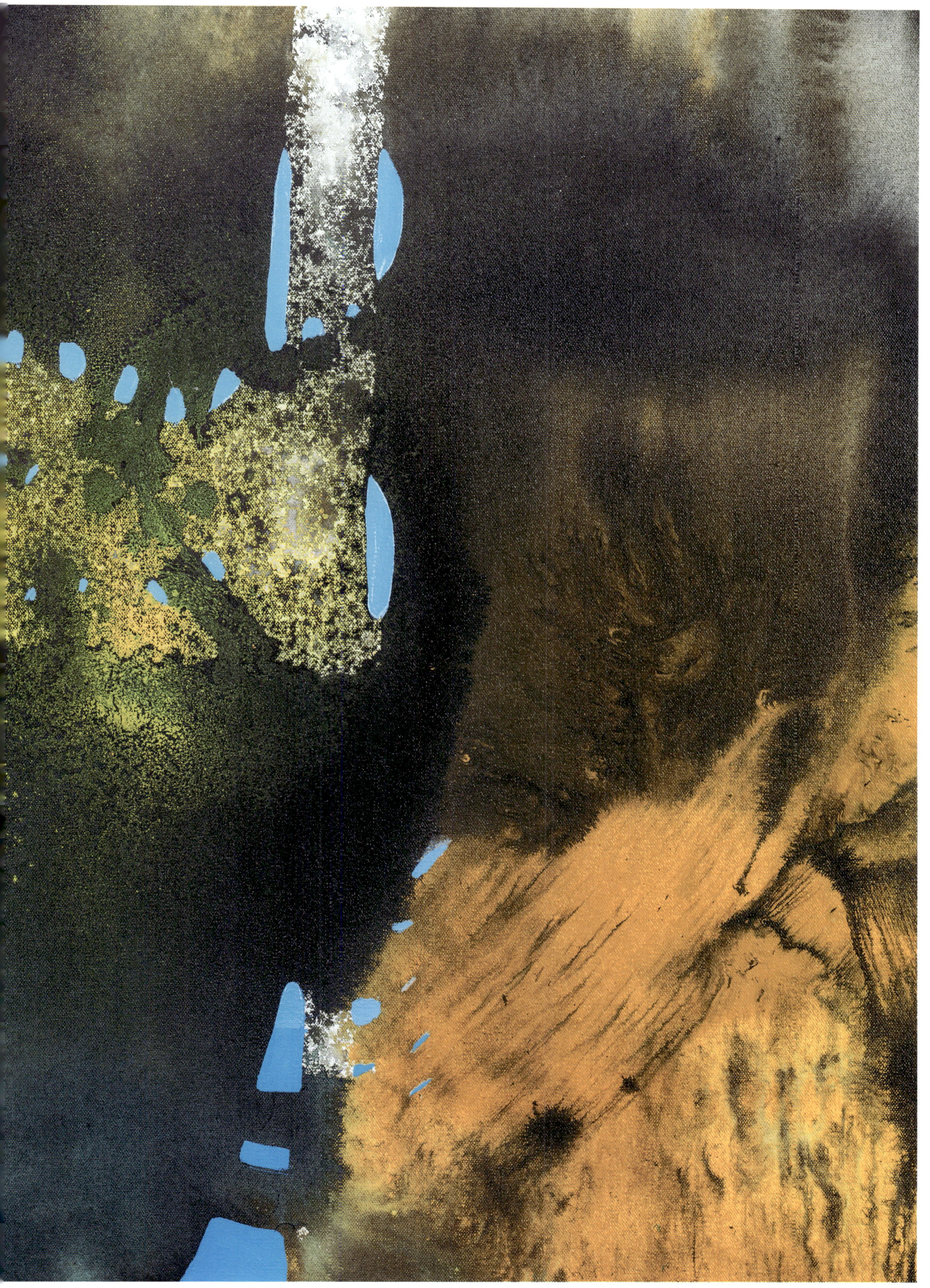

Outerworlds

Outerworld I, 2021
Oil, acrylic, and pigment on canvas, 60 in. × 48 in. (152.4 cm × 122 cm)

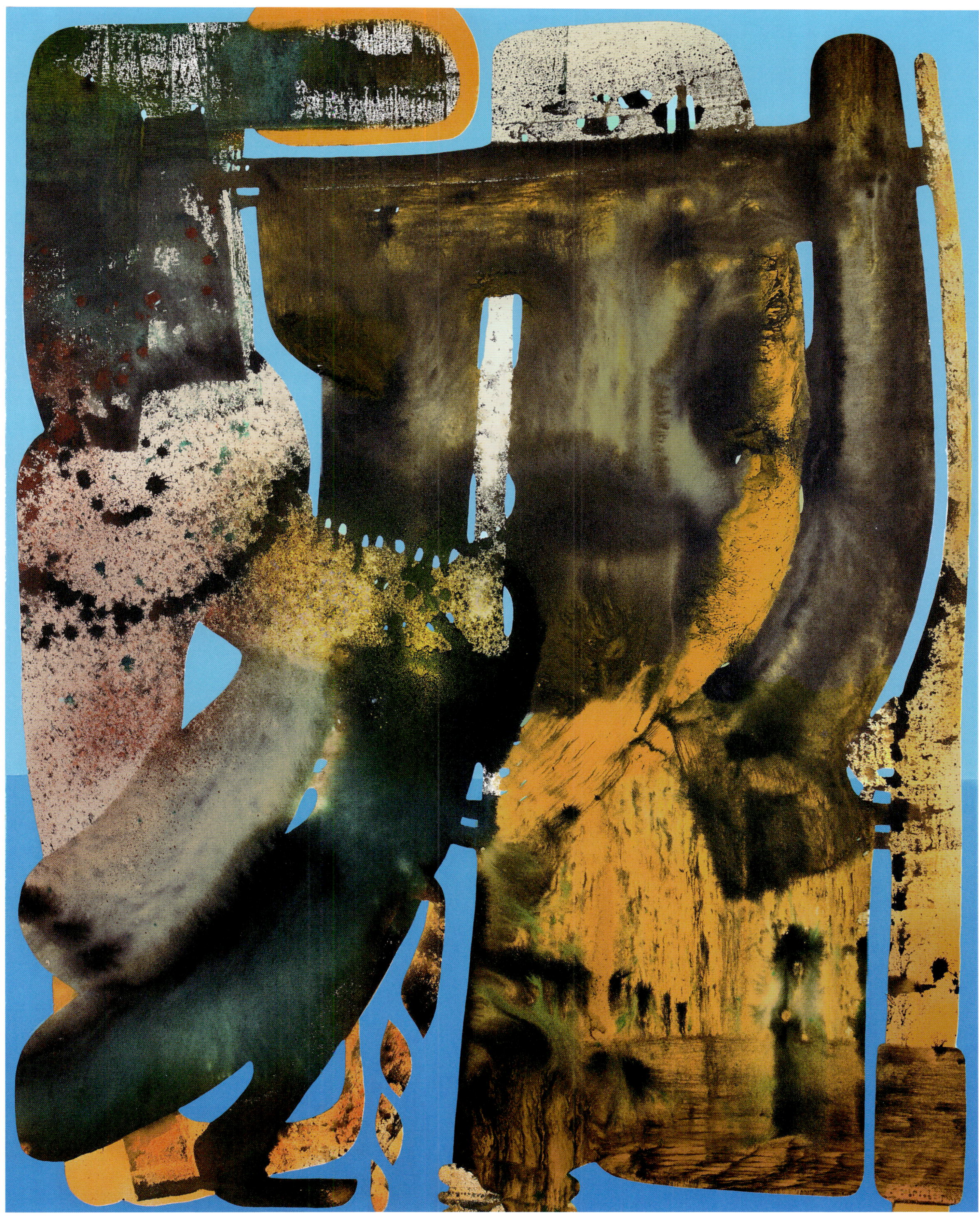

Cobra Lily, 2020
Oil, acrylic, and pigment on canvas, 79 in. × 59 in. (200.7 cm × 150 cm).

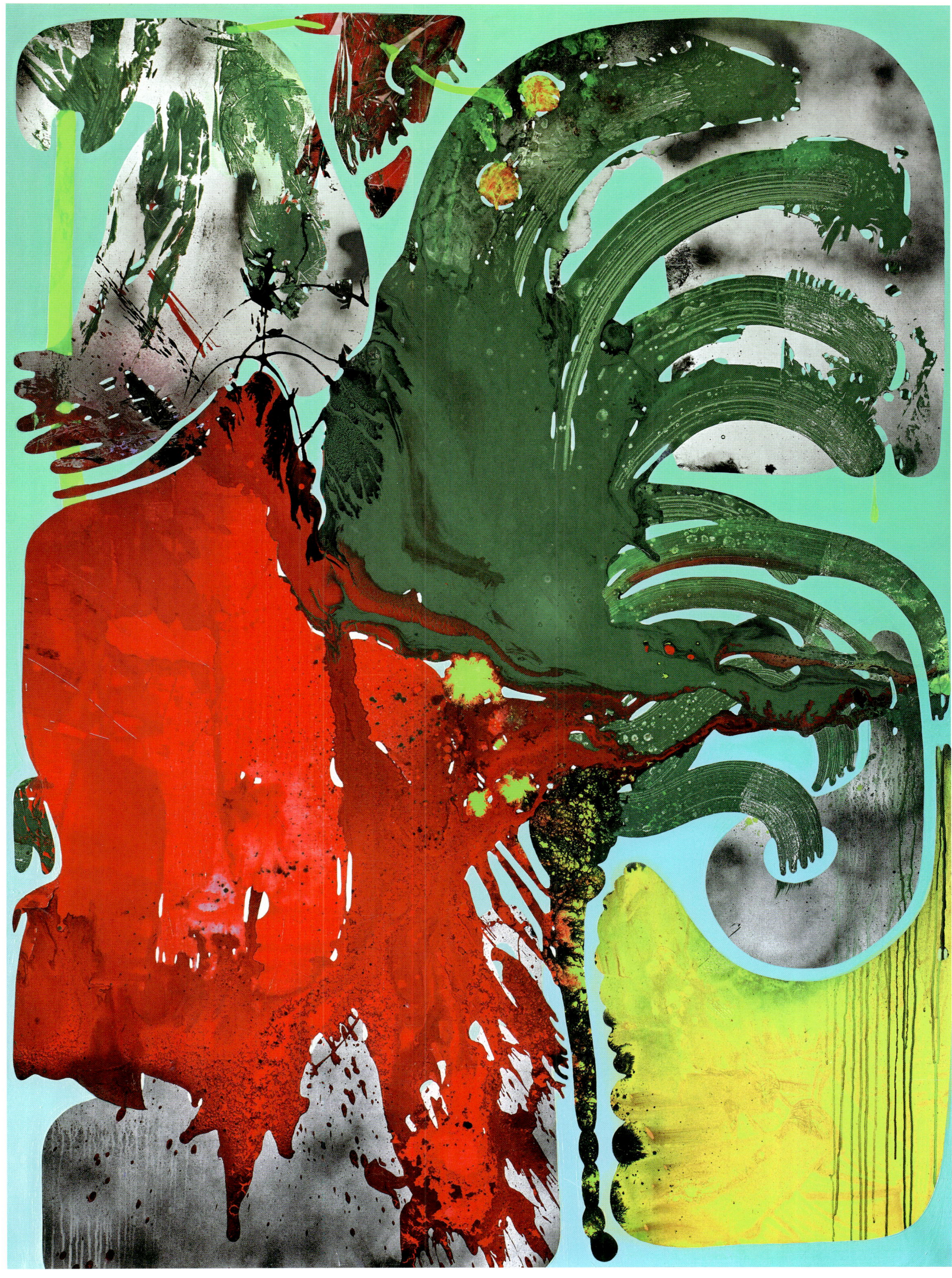

Antibodies, 2020
Acrylic on paper, 16 in. × 20 in. (40.6 cm × 50.8 cm).

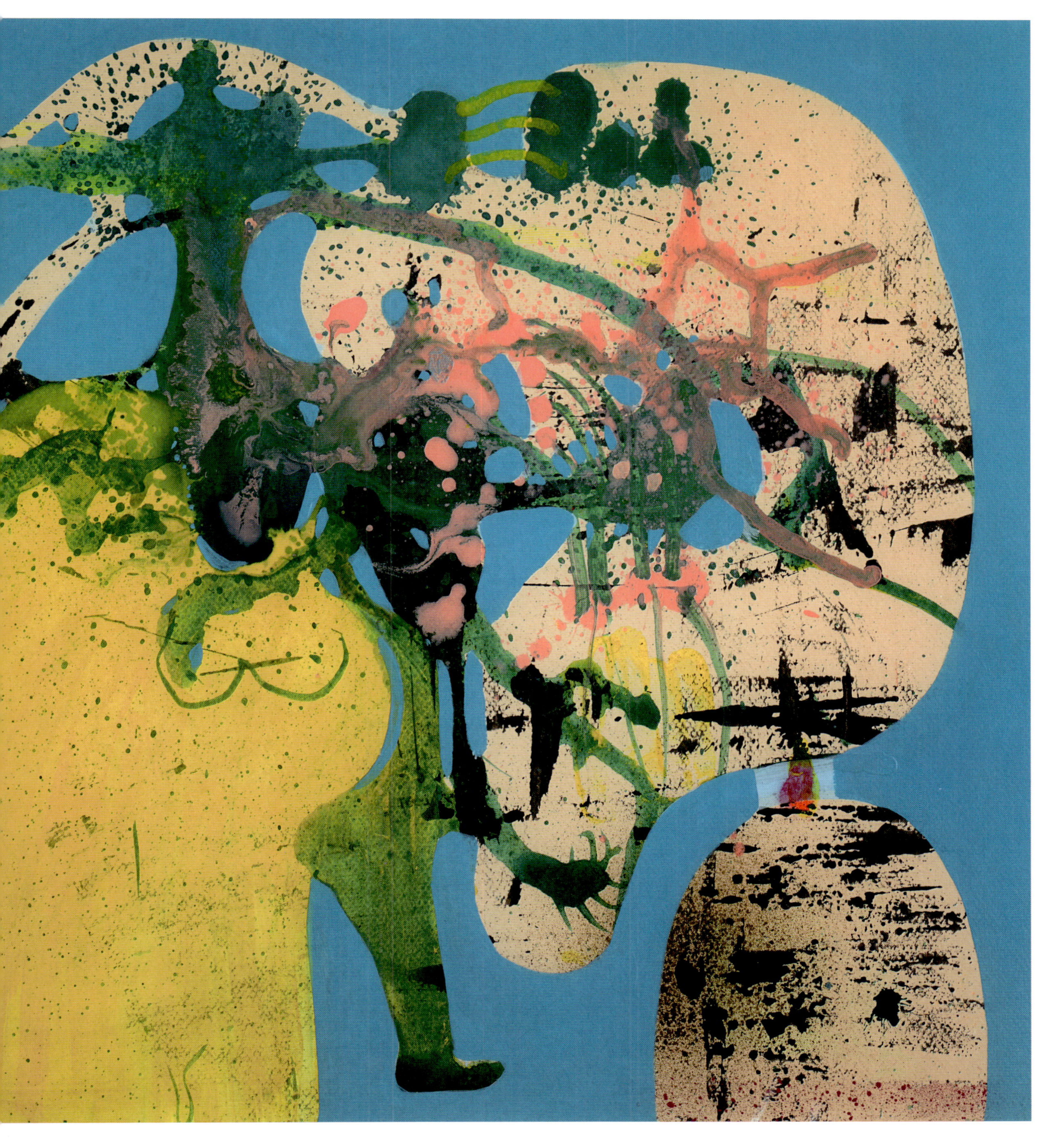

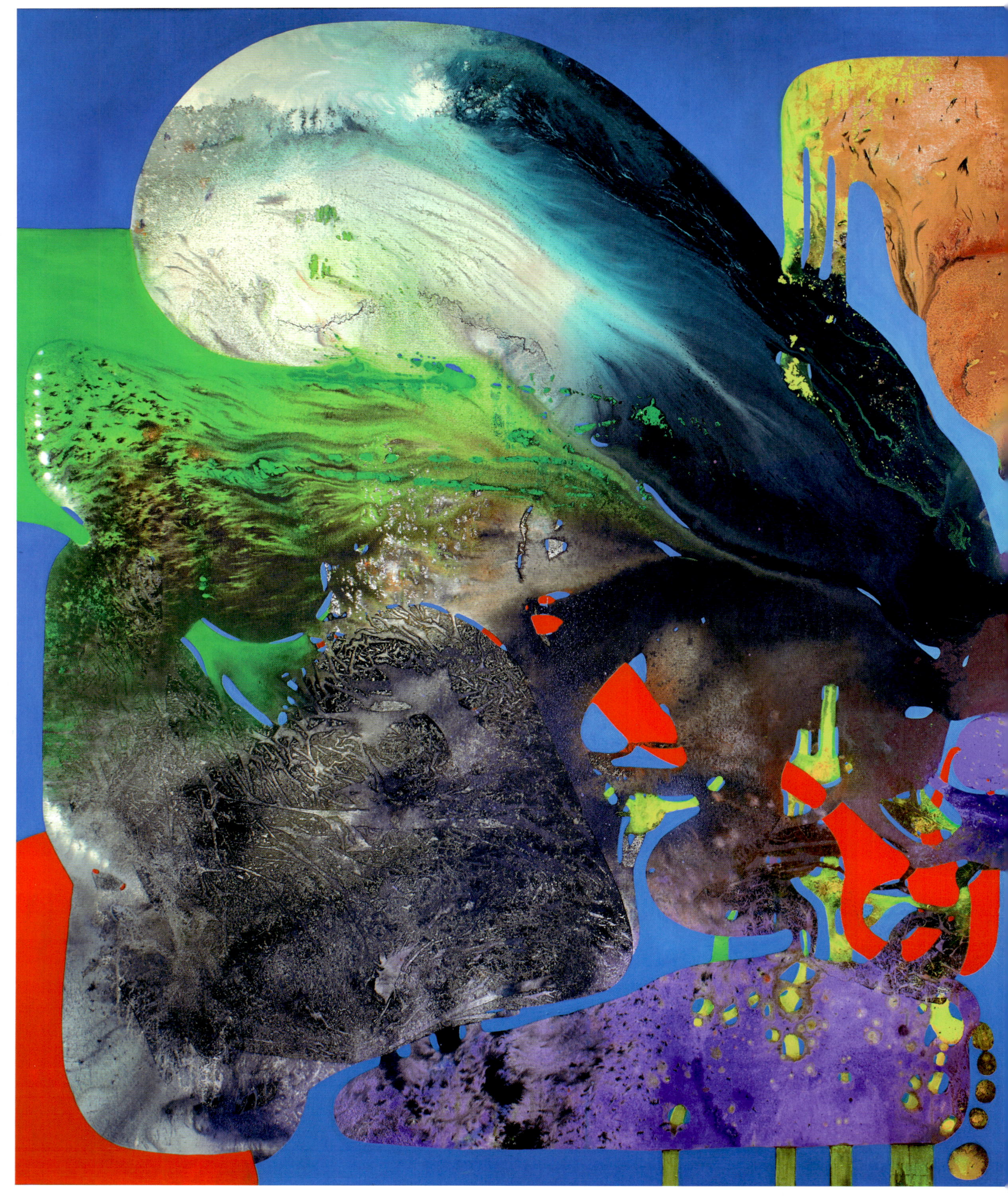

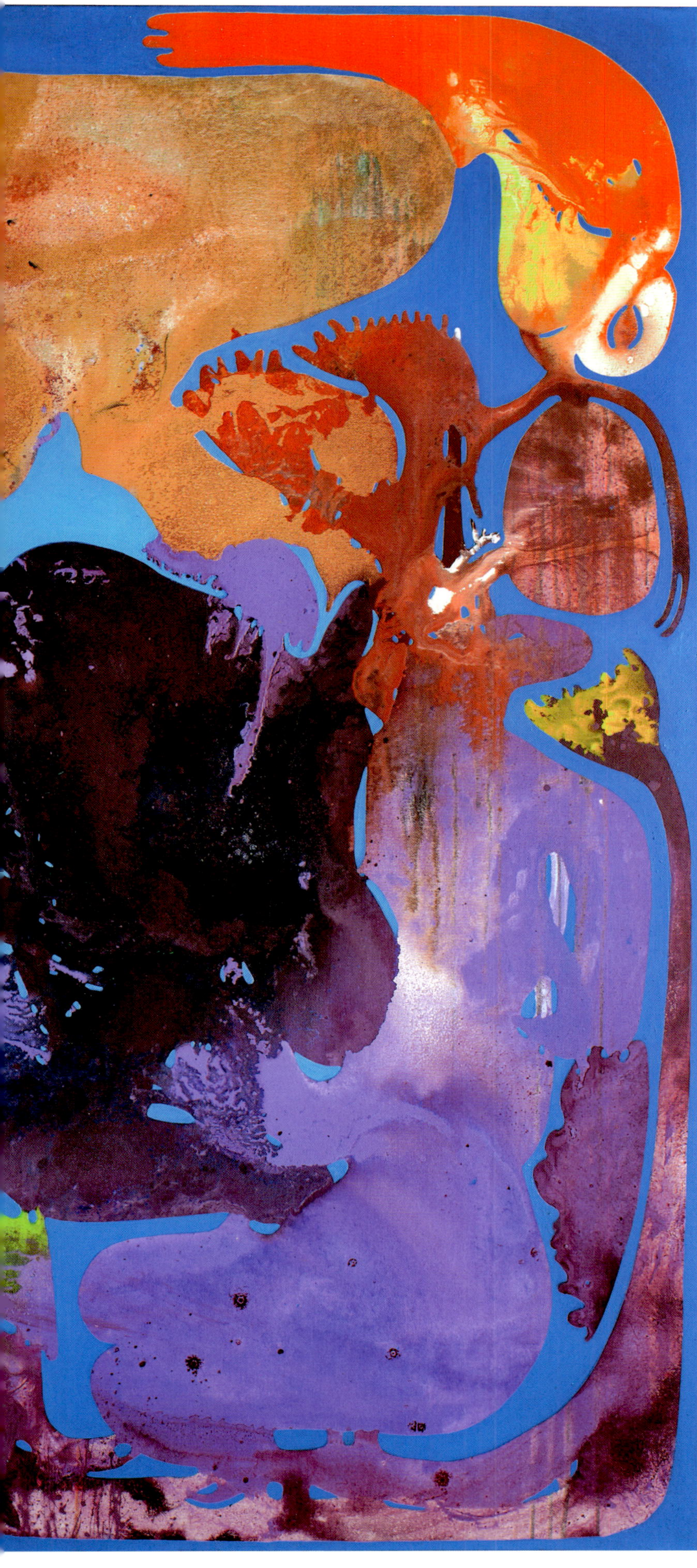

Floodgates, 2021
Oil, acrylic, and pigment on canvas, 72 in. × 96 in.
(182.9 cm × 243.8 cm)

Dilmun, 2022
Oil, acrylic, and pigment on canvas, 80 in. × 60 in. (203.2 cm × 152.4 cm)

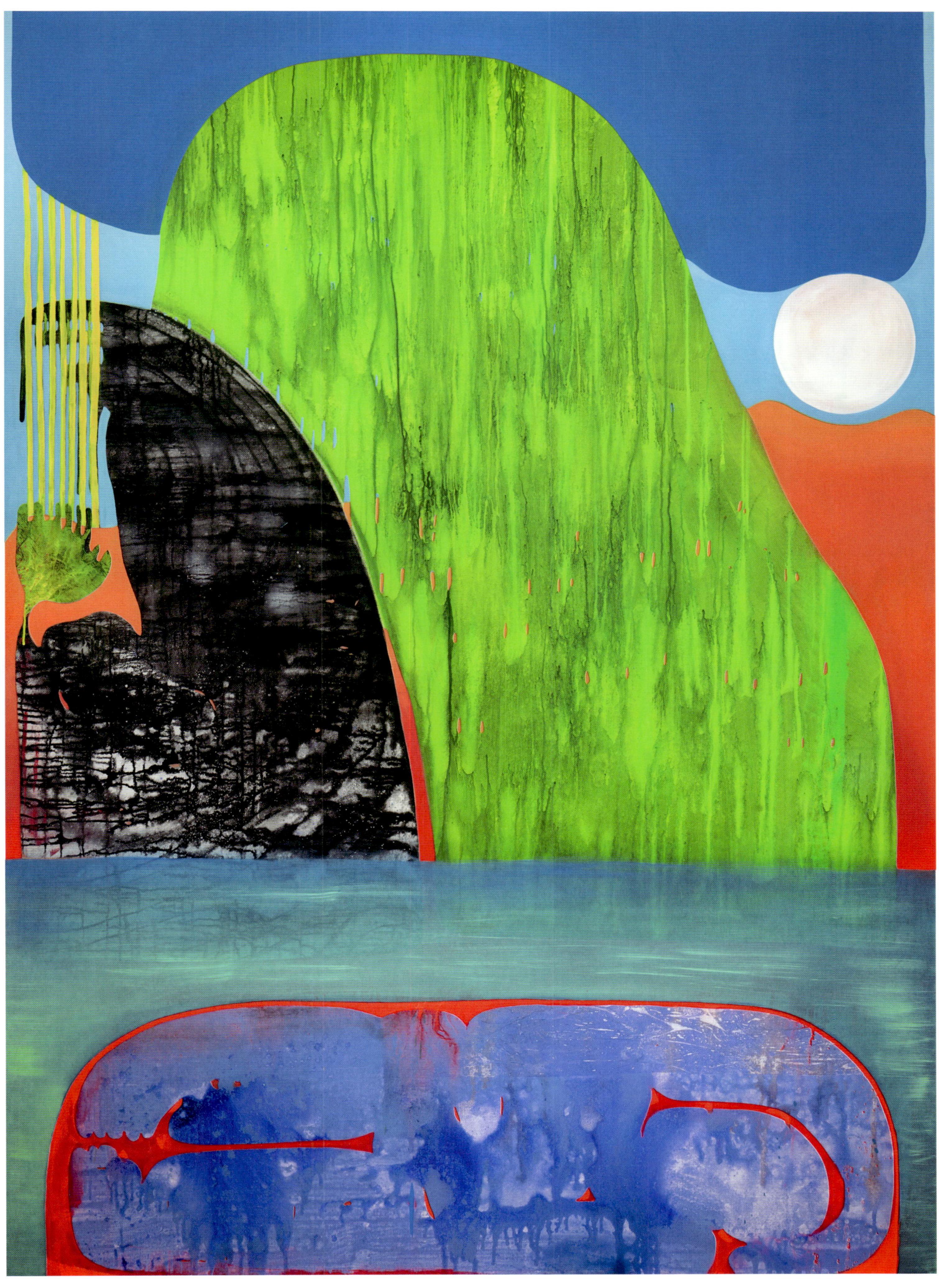

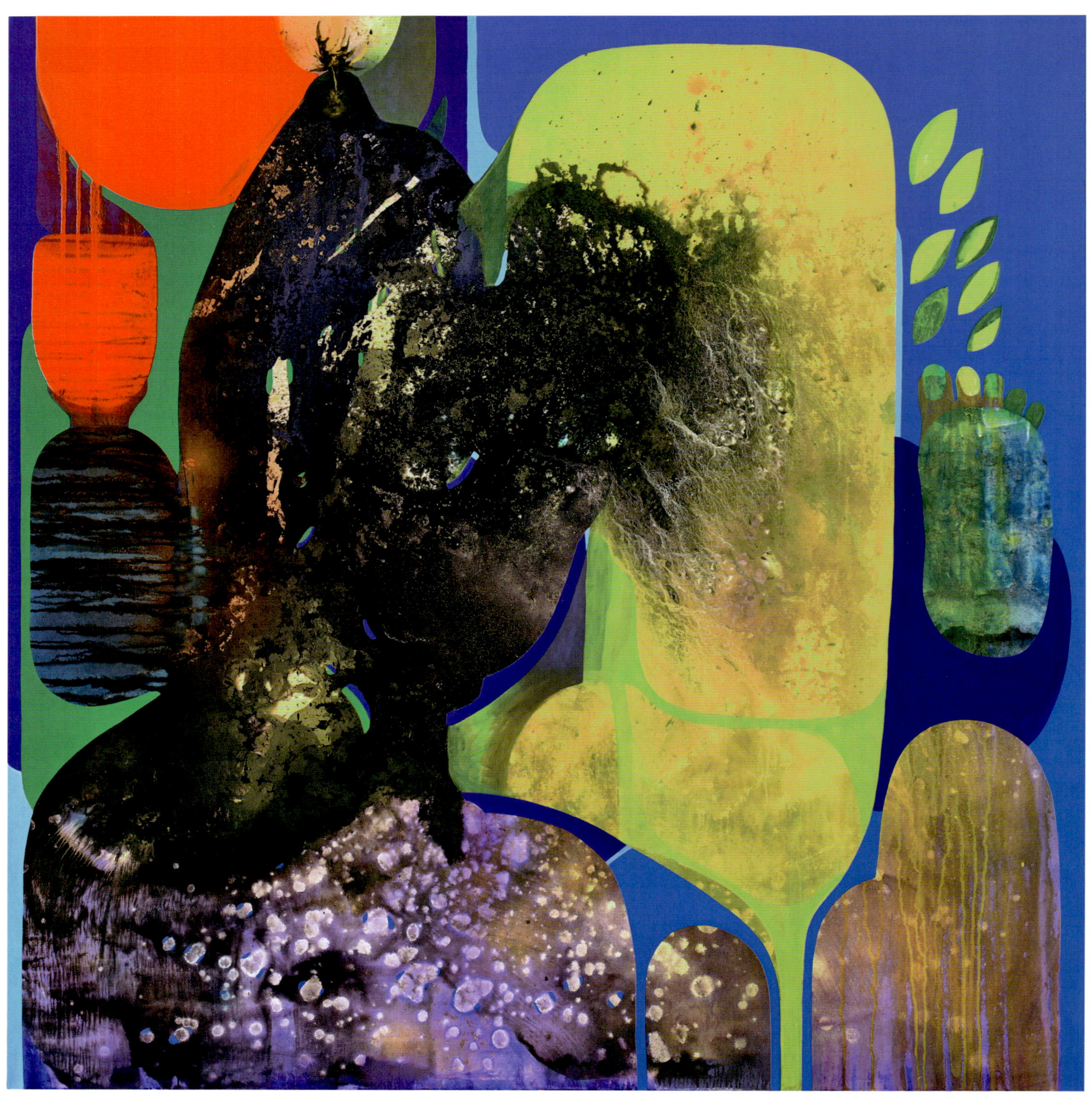

Sanctum, 2023
Oil, acrylic, and pigment on canvas, 62 in. × 62 in. (157.5 cm × 157.5 cm)

Echo and Narcissus, 2018
Oil, acrylic, and pigment on canvas, 84 in. × 60 in.
(213.4 cm × 152.4 cm)

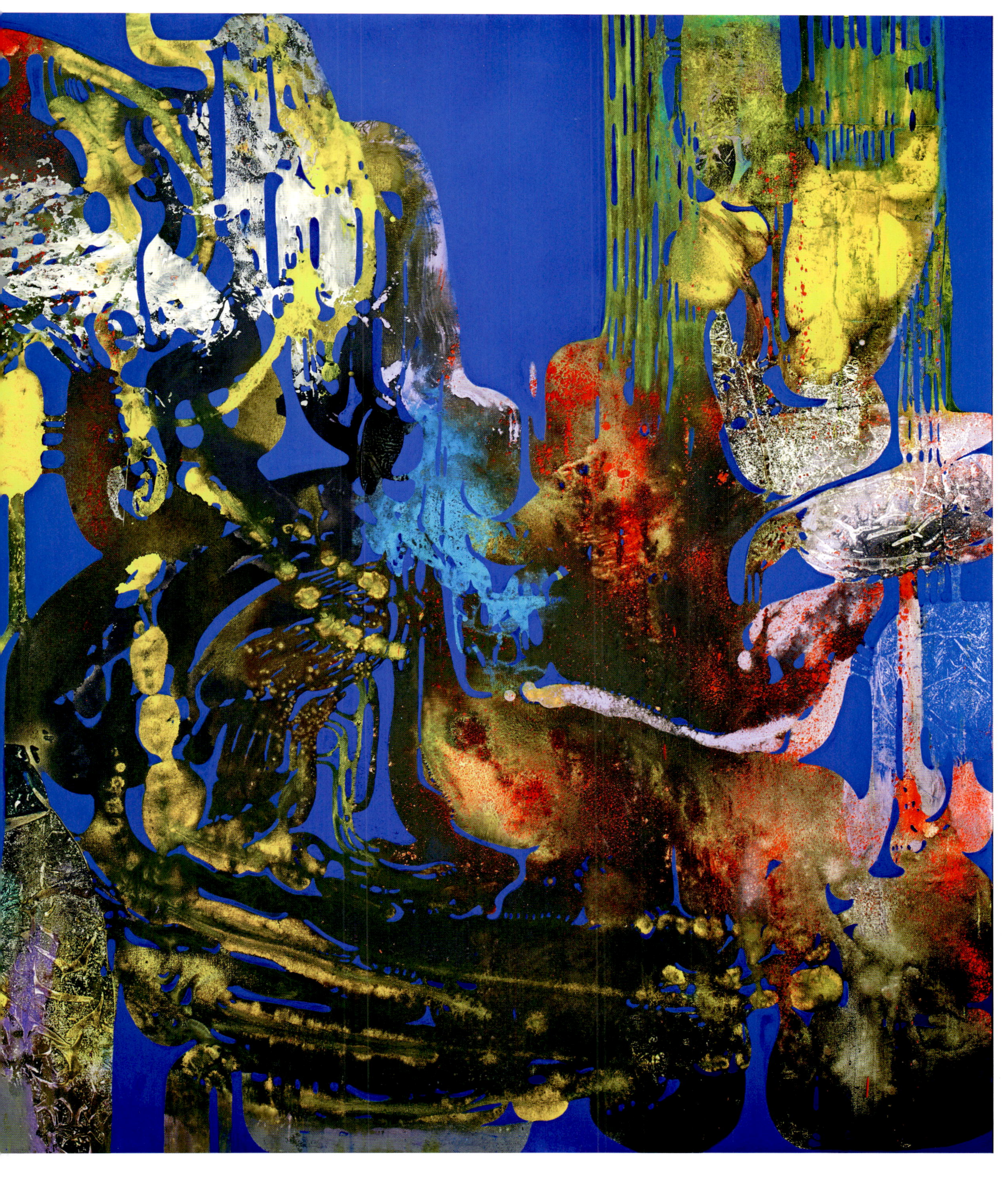

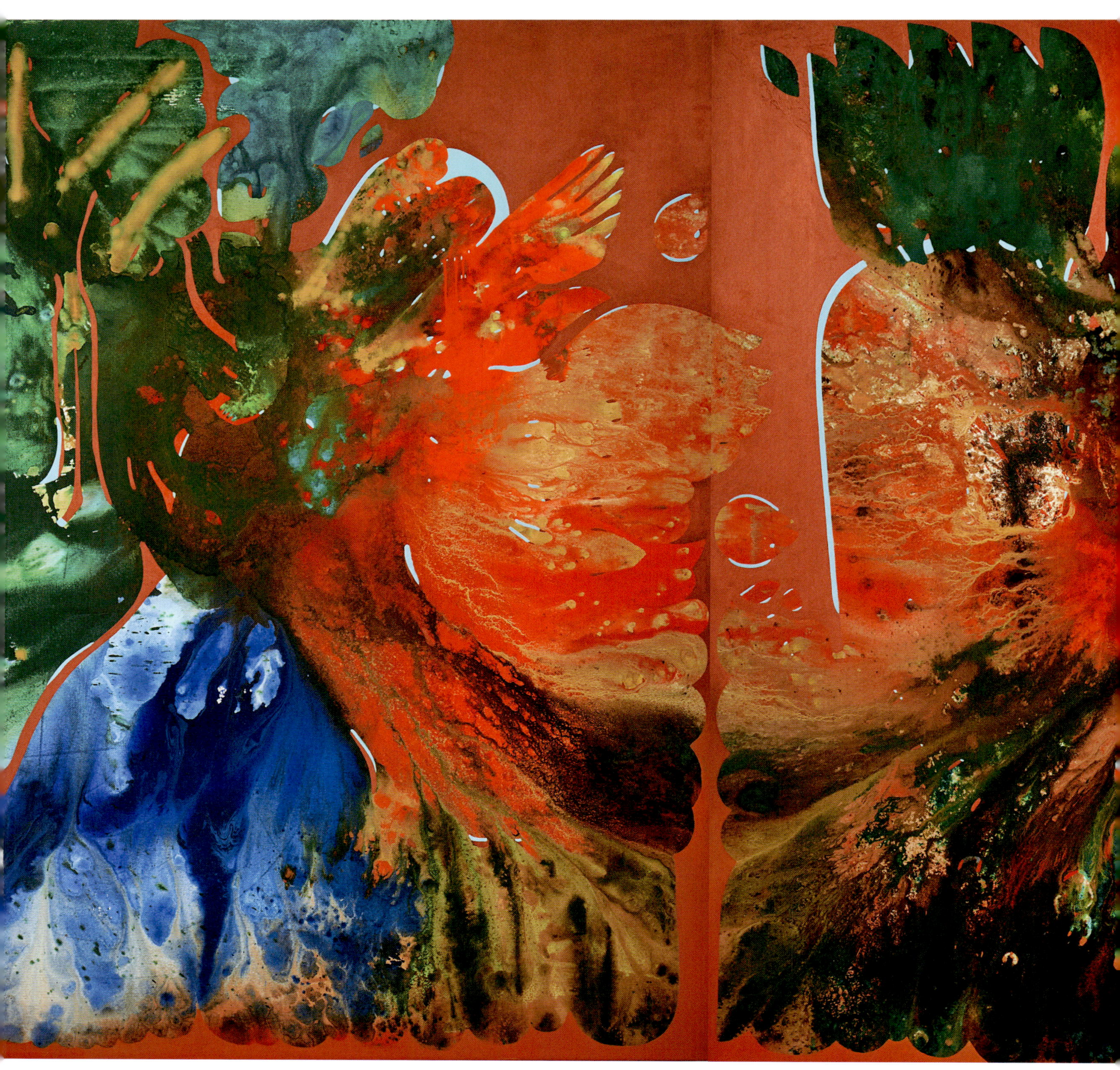

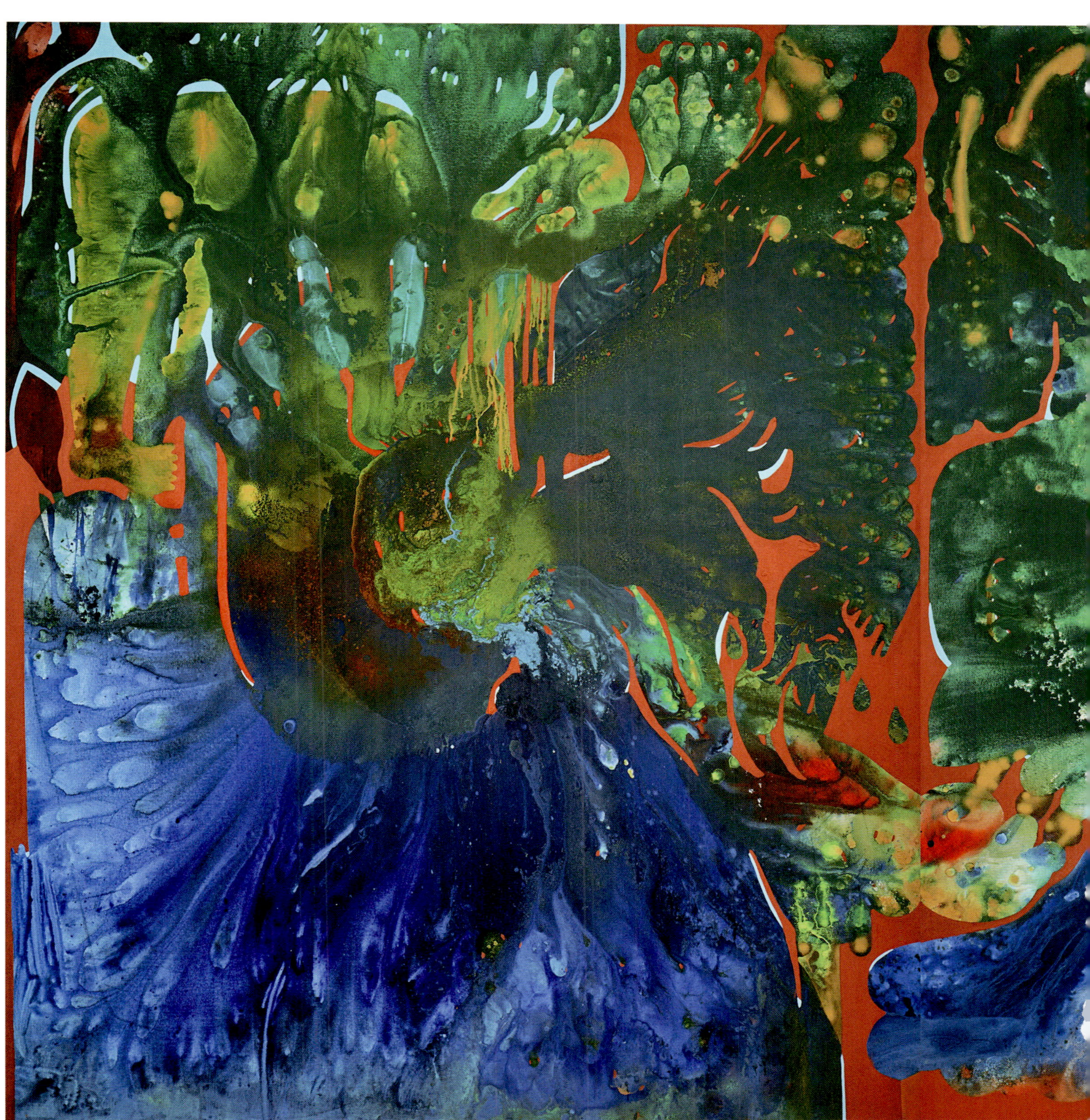

Abzu, 2023
Oil, acrylic, and pigment on canvas, 84 ft. × 29 ½ ft. (2.13 m × 8.89 m)

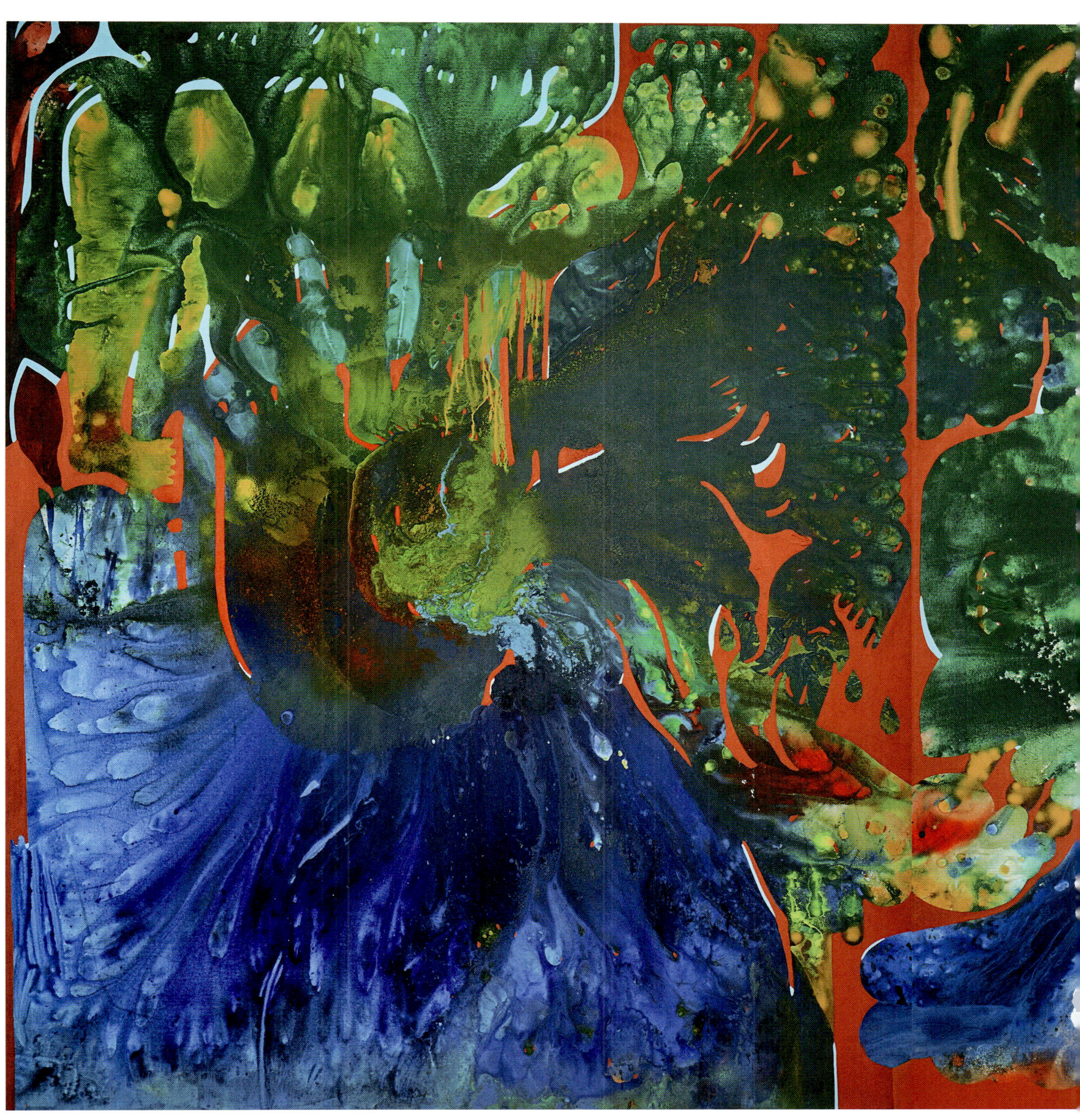

Abzu, 2023
Oil, acrylic, and pigment on canvas, 84 ft. × 29 ½ ft. (2.13 m × 8.89 m)

Pages 50 and 51

Abzu, panels 1 and 4

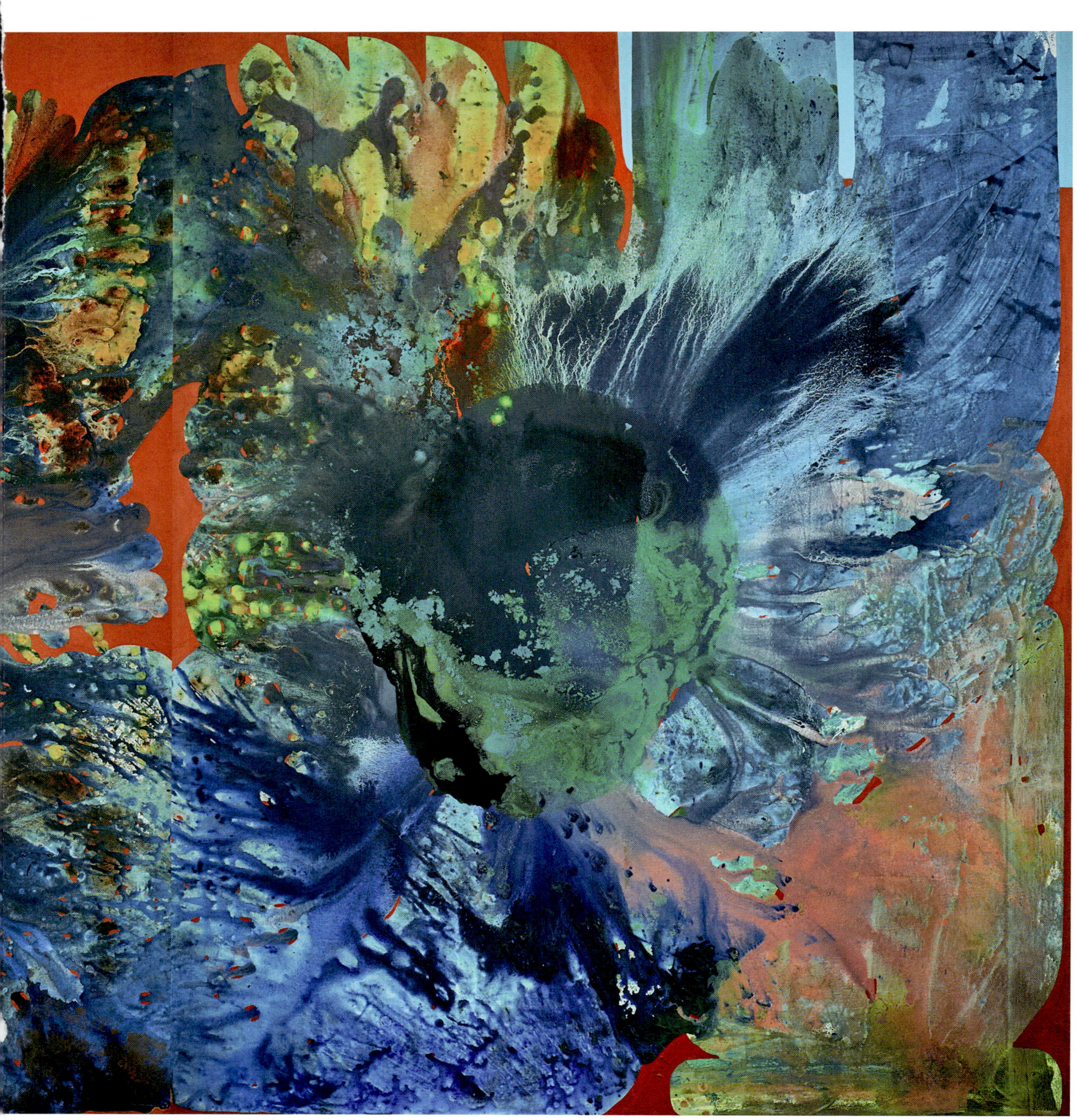

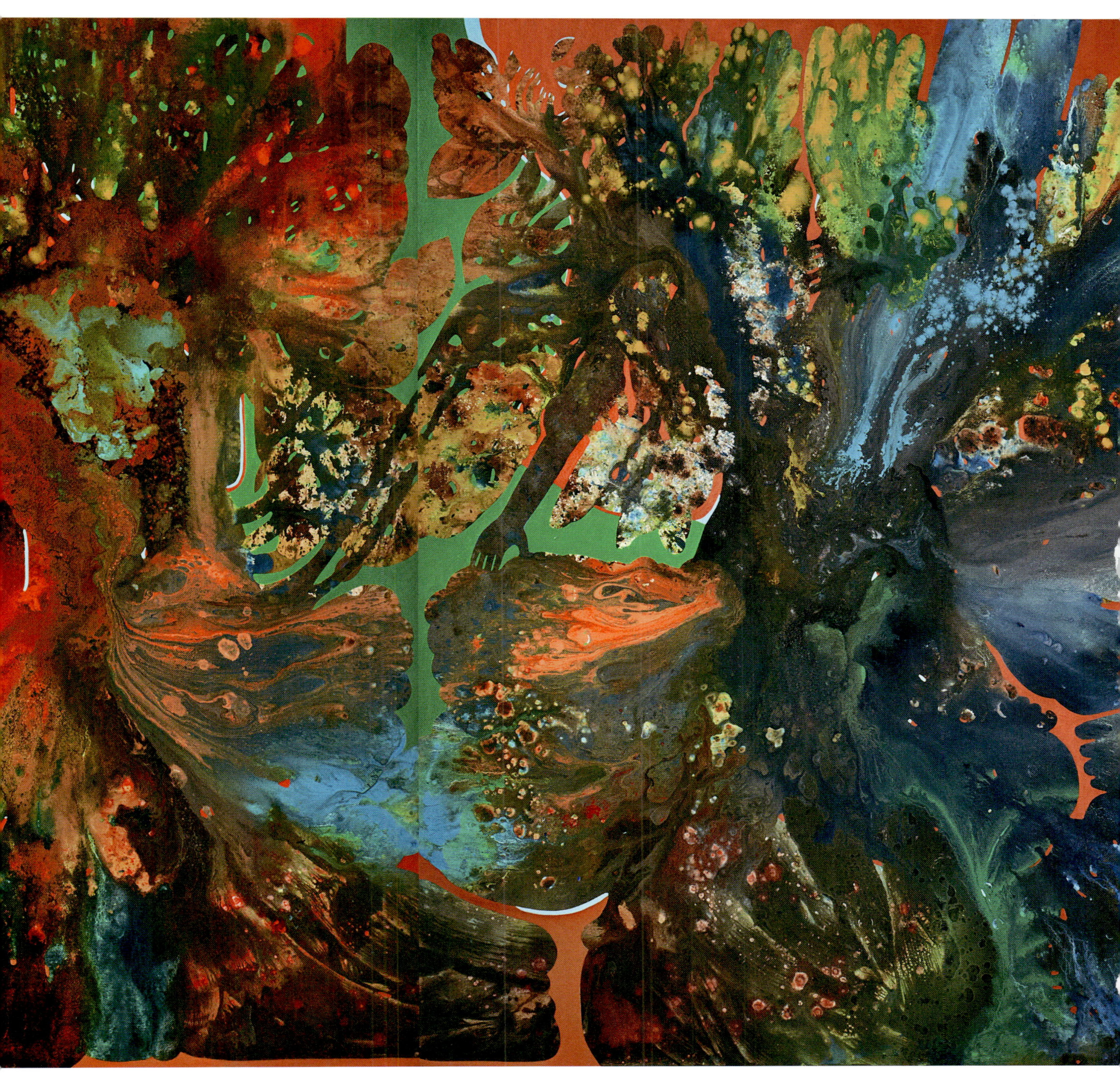

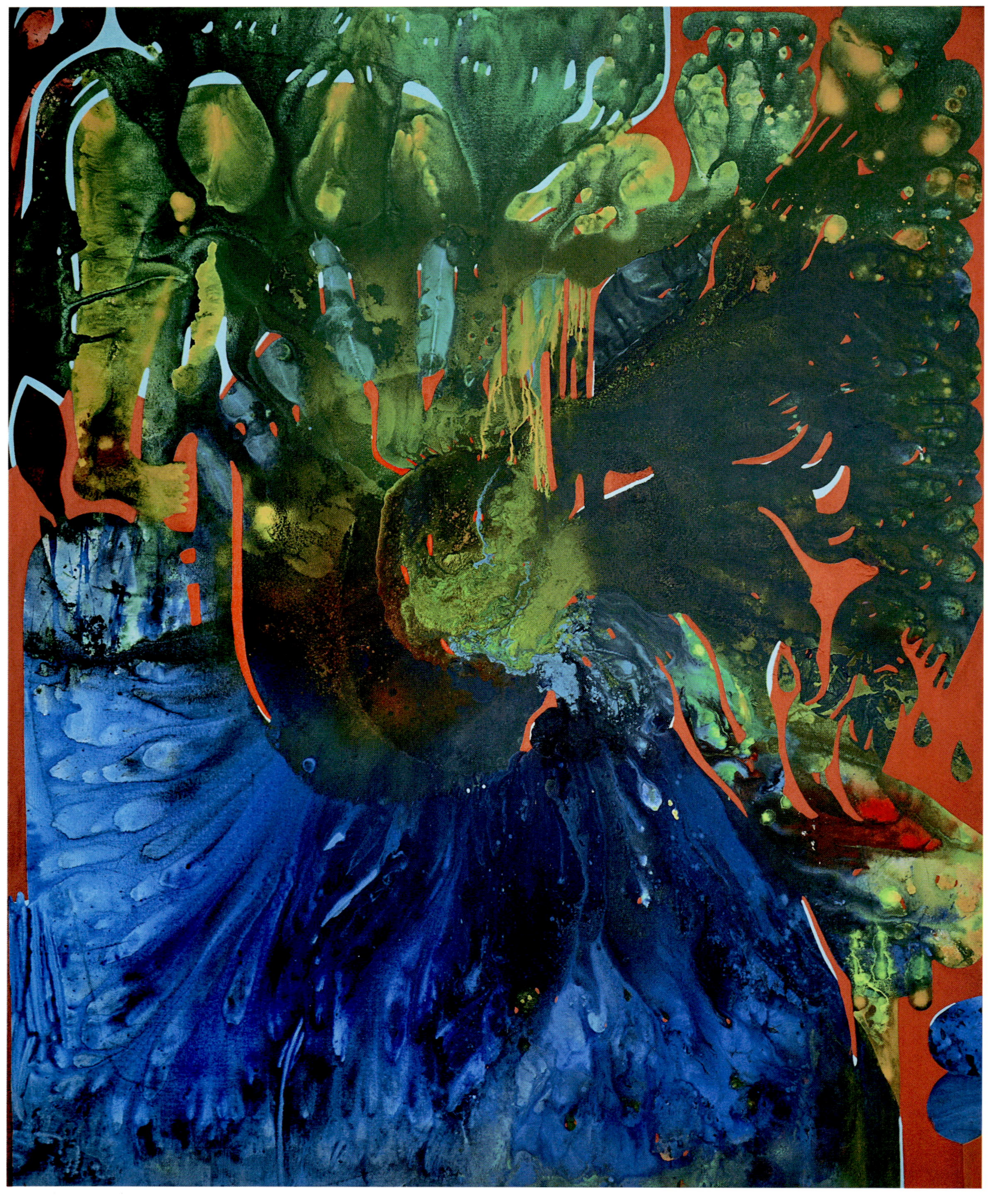

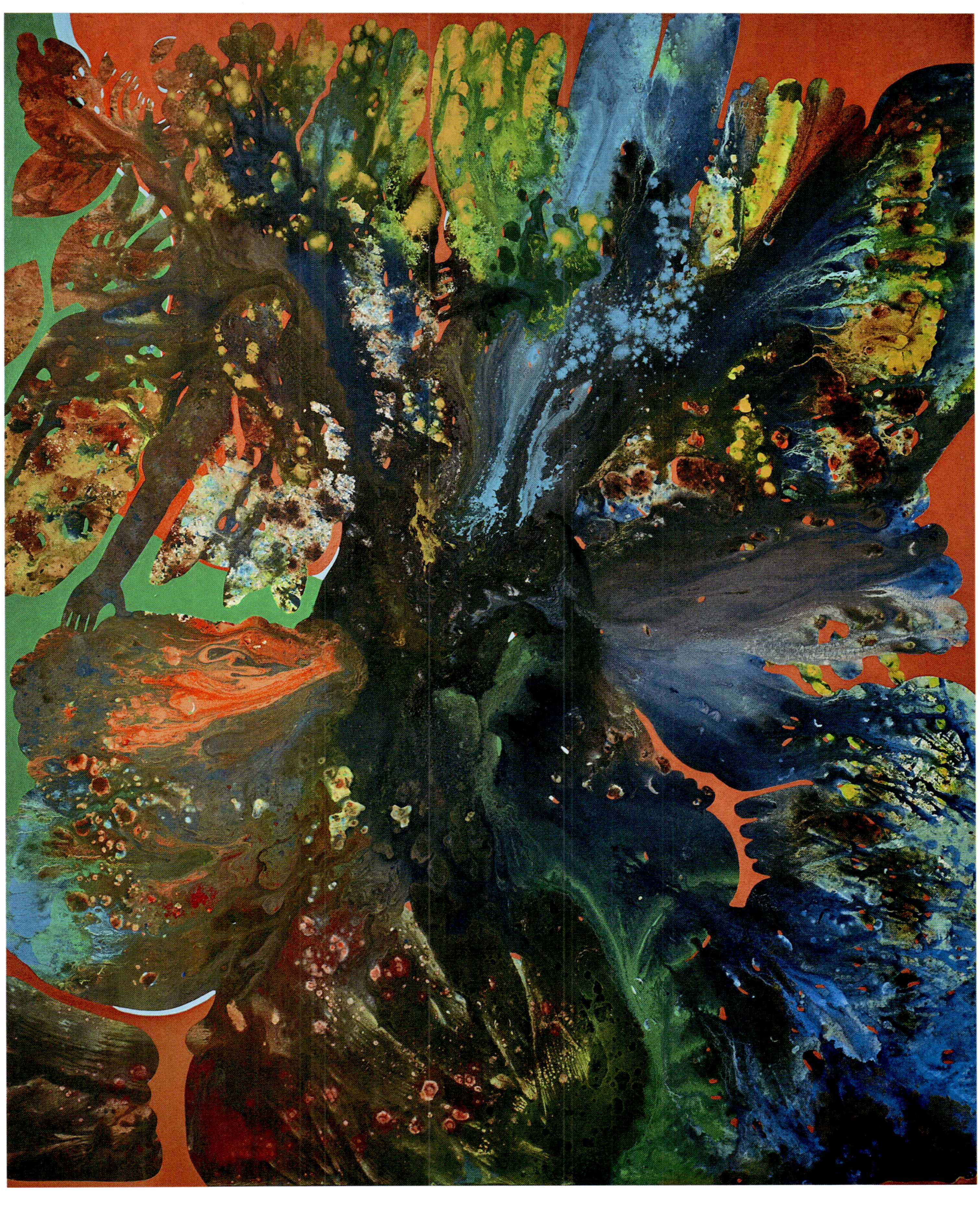

Citizen, 2019.
Oil, acrylic, and pigment on canvas, 48 in. × 48 in. (122 cm × 122 cm)

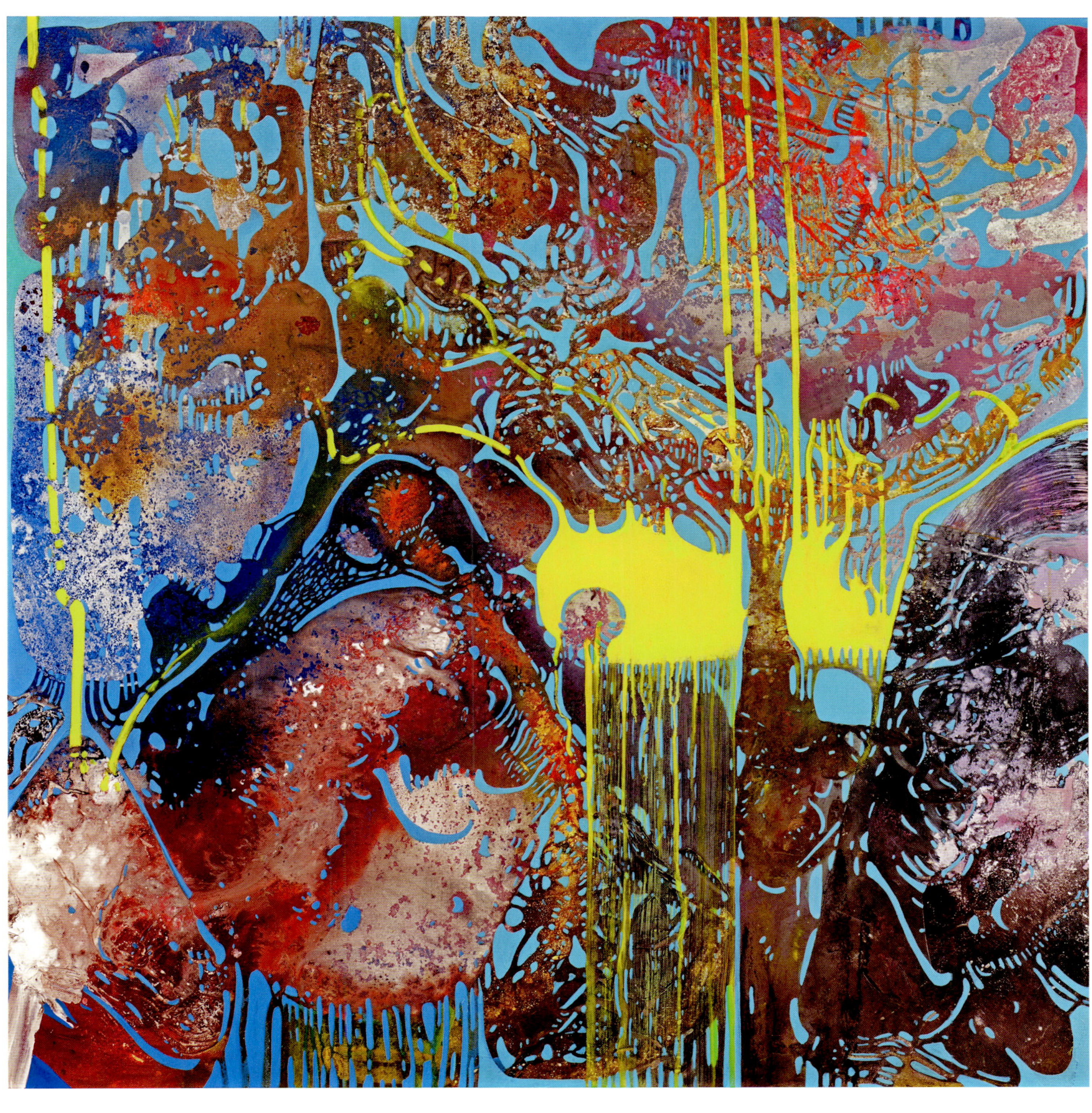

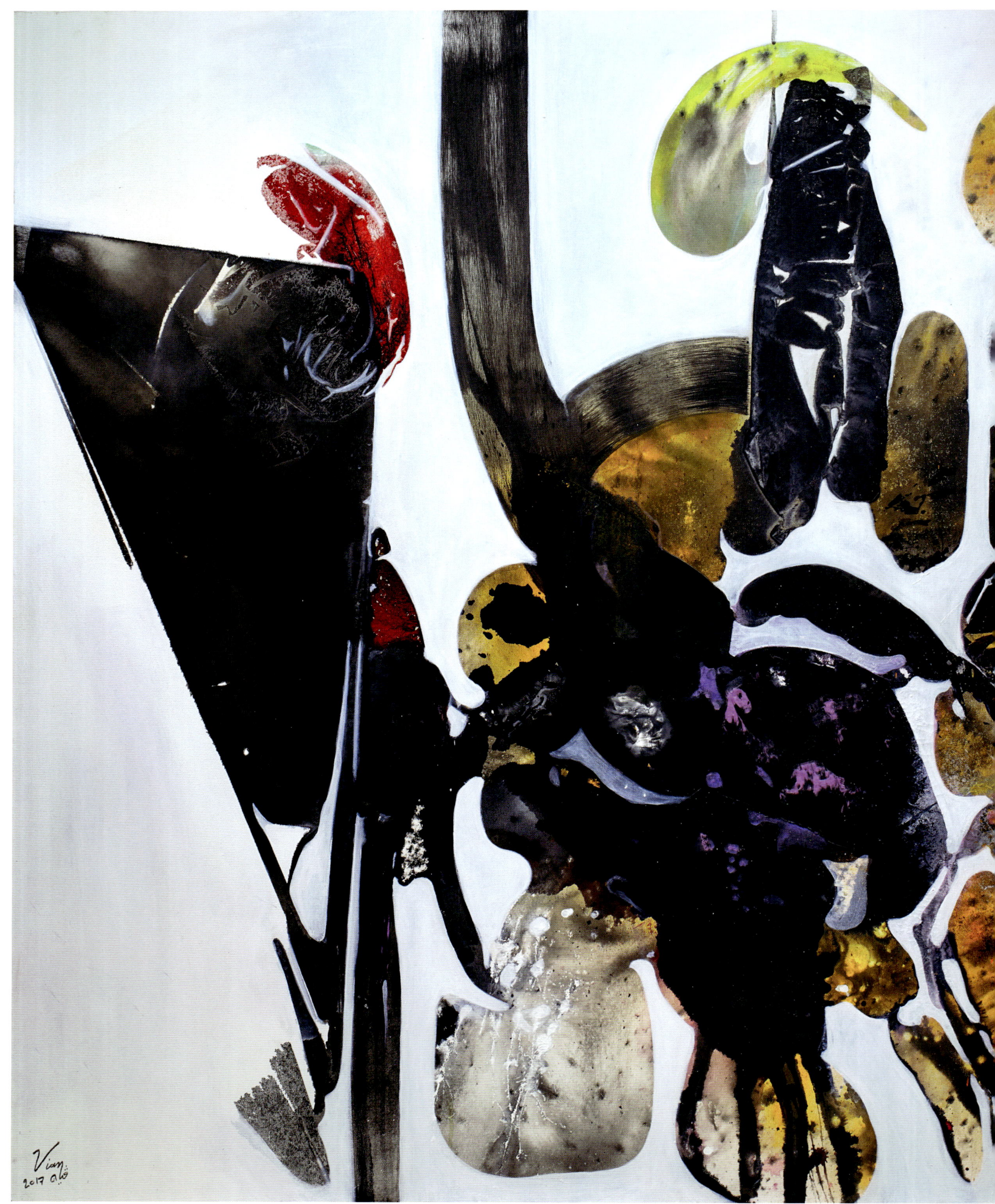
Vian
2017

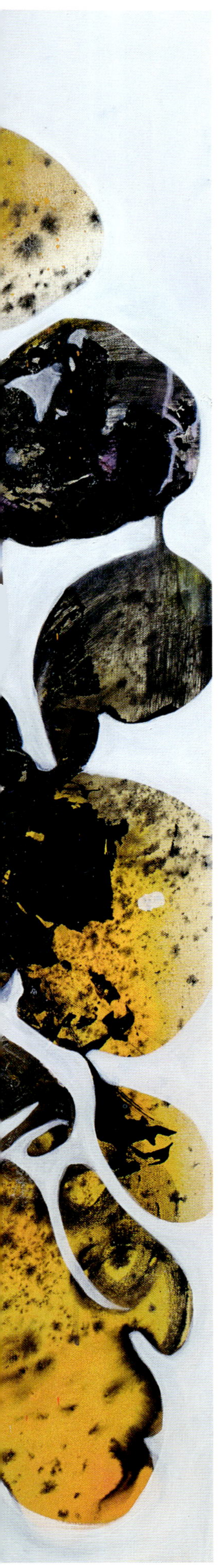

Landscape with a Moth, 2016
Oil, acrylic, and pigment on canvas, 48 in. × 48 in. (122 cm × 122 cm)

Woodlands, 2020
Oil, acrylic, and pigment on canvas, 72 in. × 60 in. (183 cm × 152.4 cm)

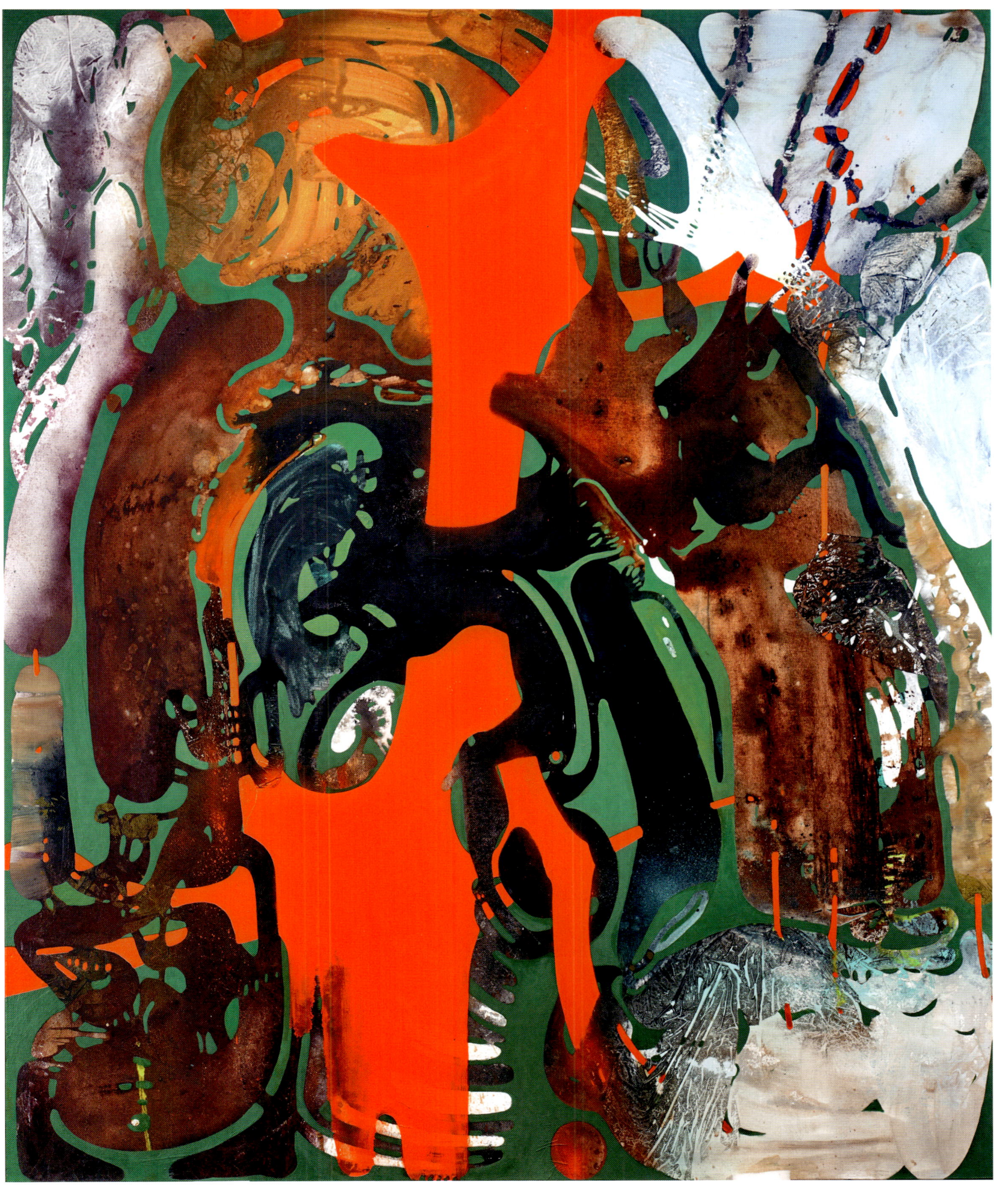

Heart Lines, 2016
Acrylic finished with oil on canvas, 60 in. × 48 in. (152.4 cm × 122 cm)

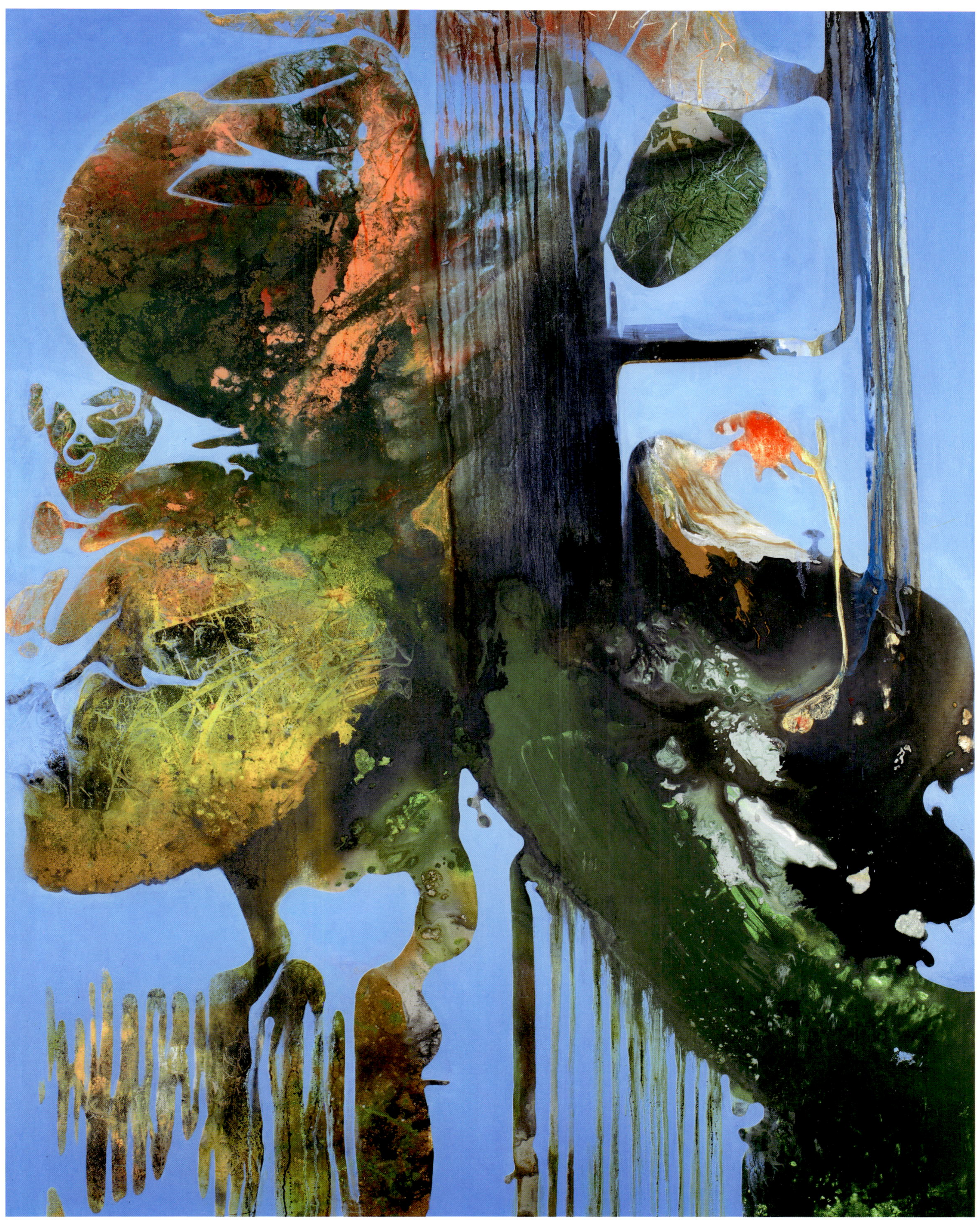

Cherry Pickers, 2022
Oil, acrylic, and pigment on canvas, 48 in. × 60 in.
(122 cm × 152.4 cm)

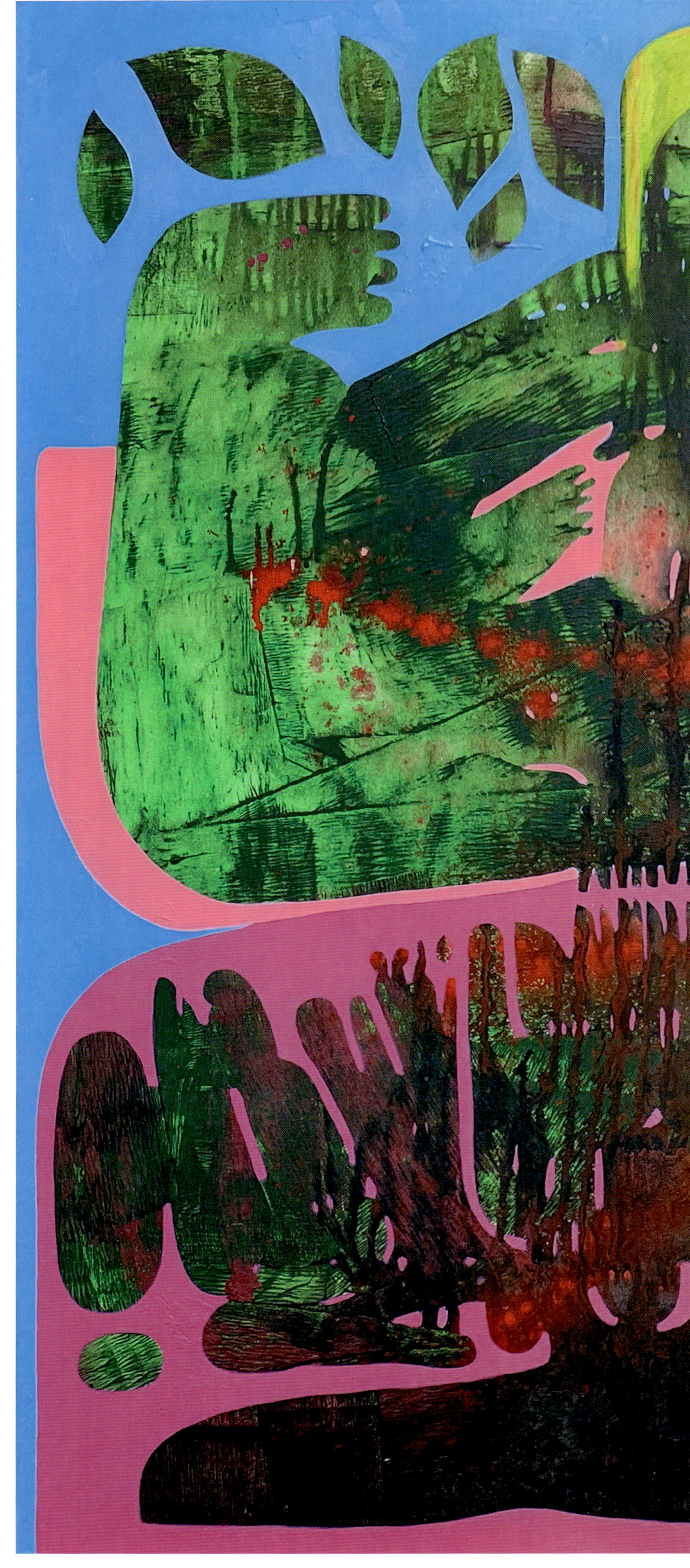

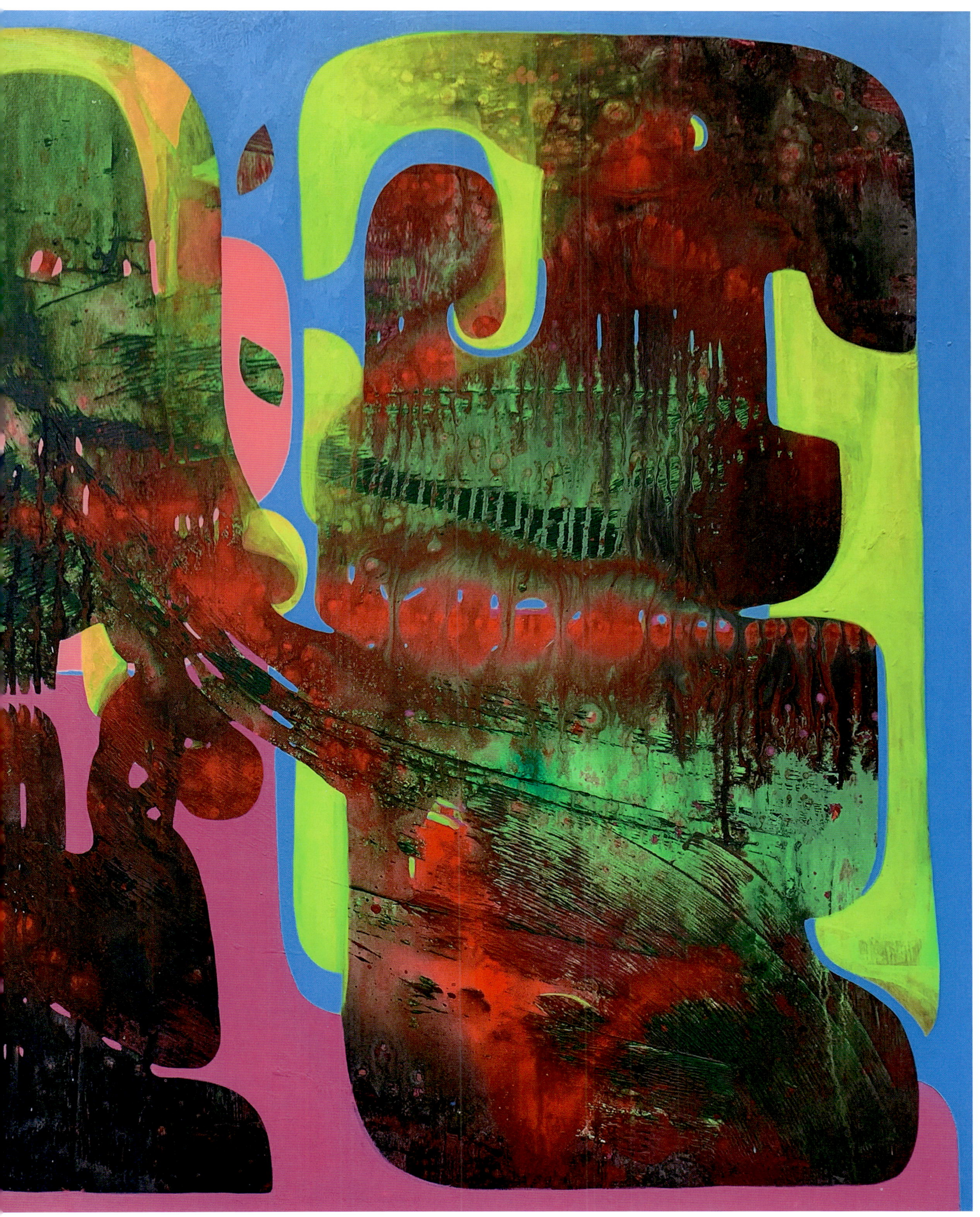

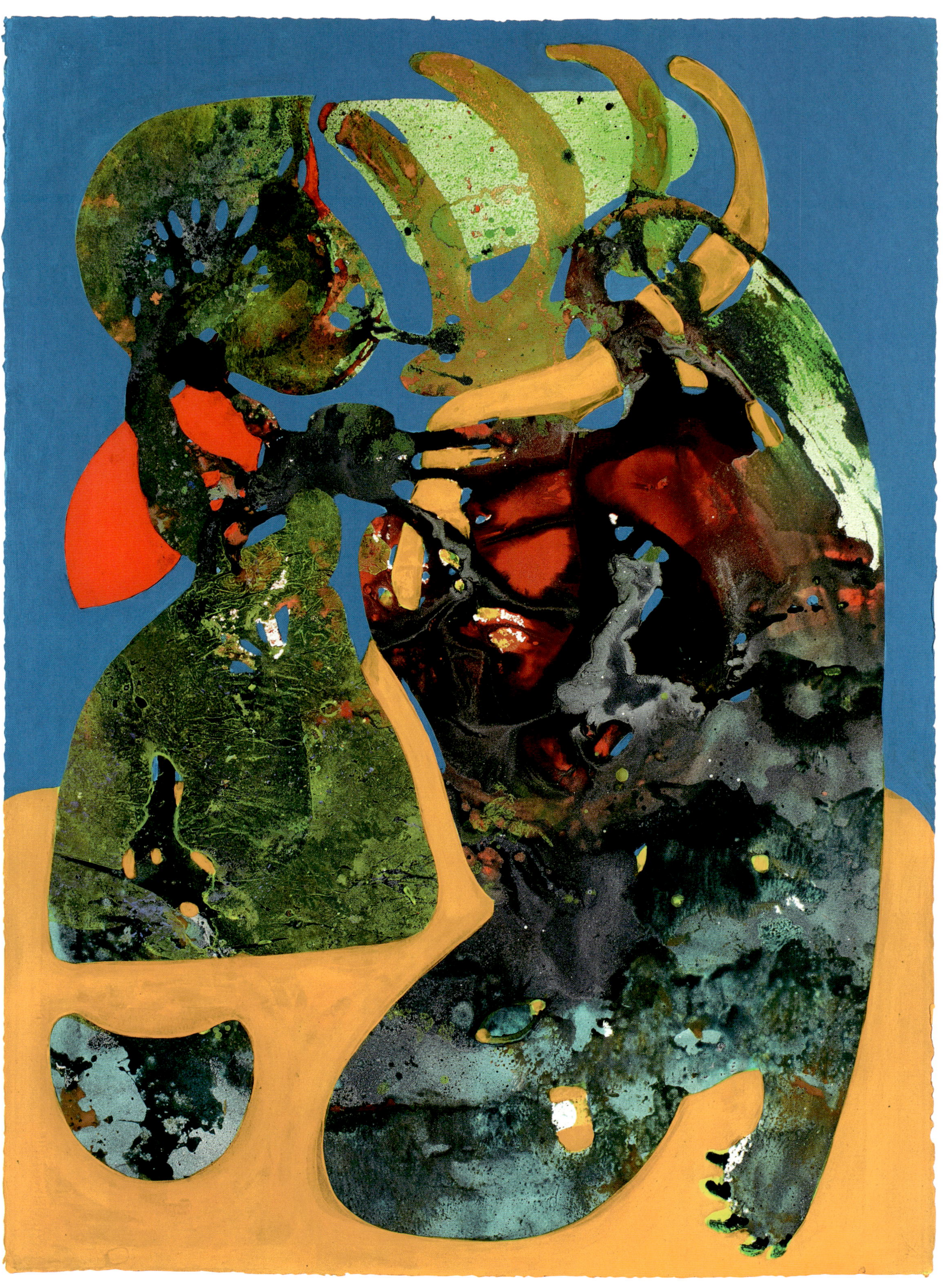

Forest Remains I, 2023
Oil, acrylic, and pigment on Arches paper, 30 in. × 22 ½ in. (76.2 cm × 57.2 cm)

Ecotone I, 2023
Oil, acrylic, and pigment on canvas, 72 in. × 67 in. (183 cm × 170.2 cm)

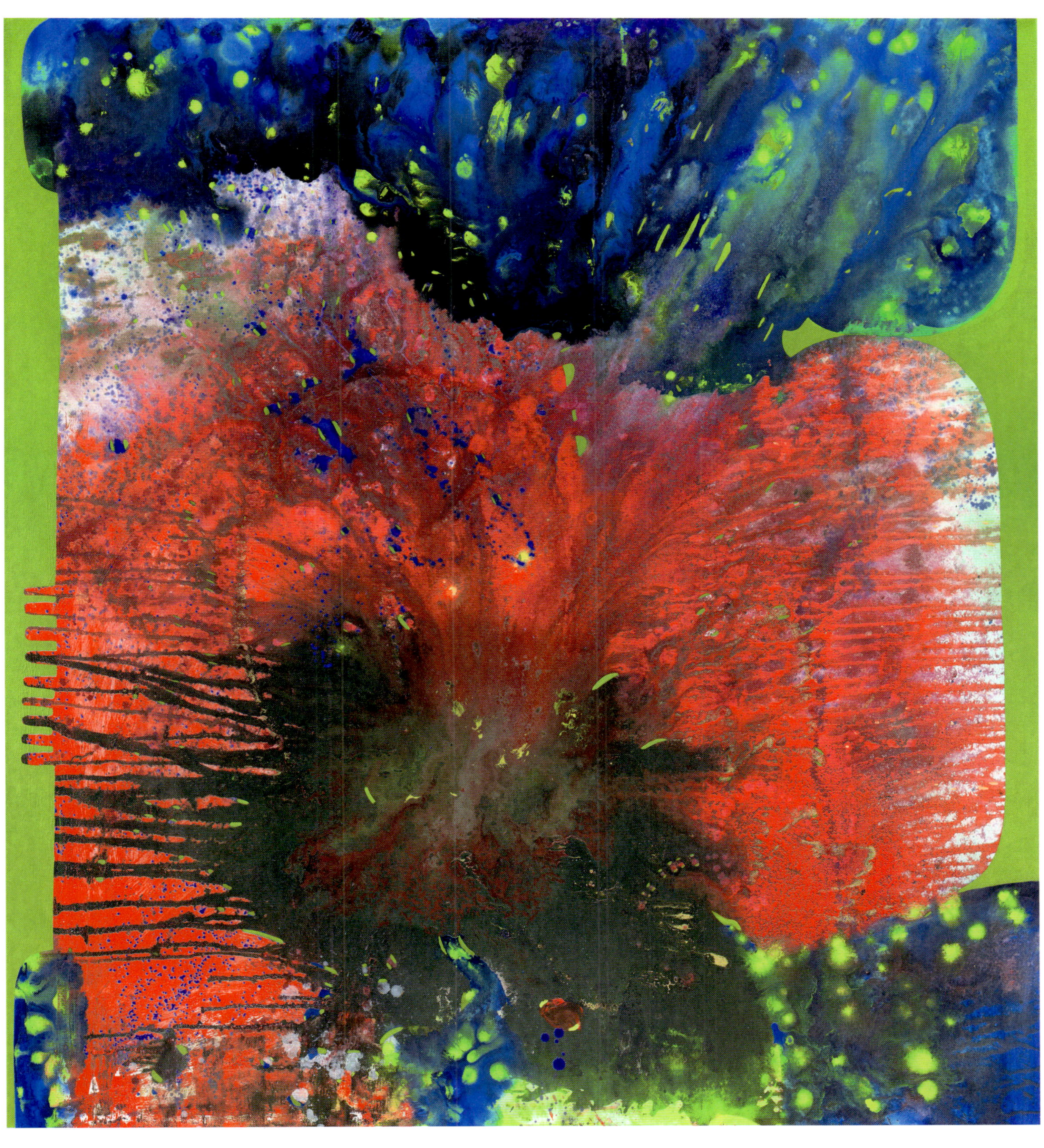

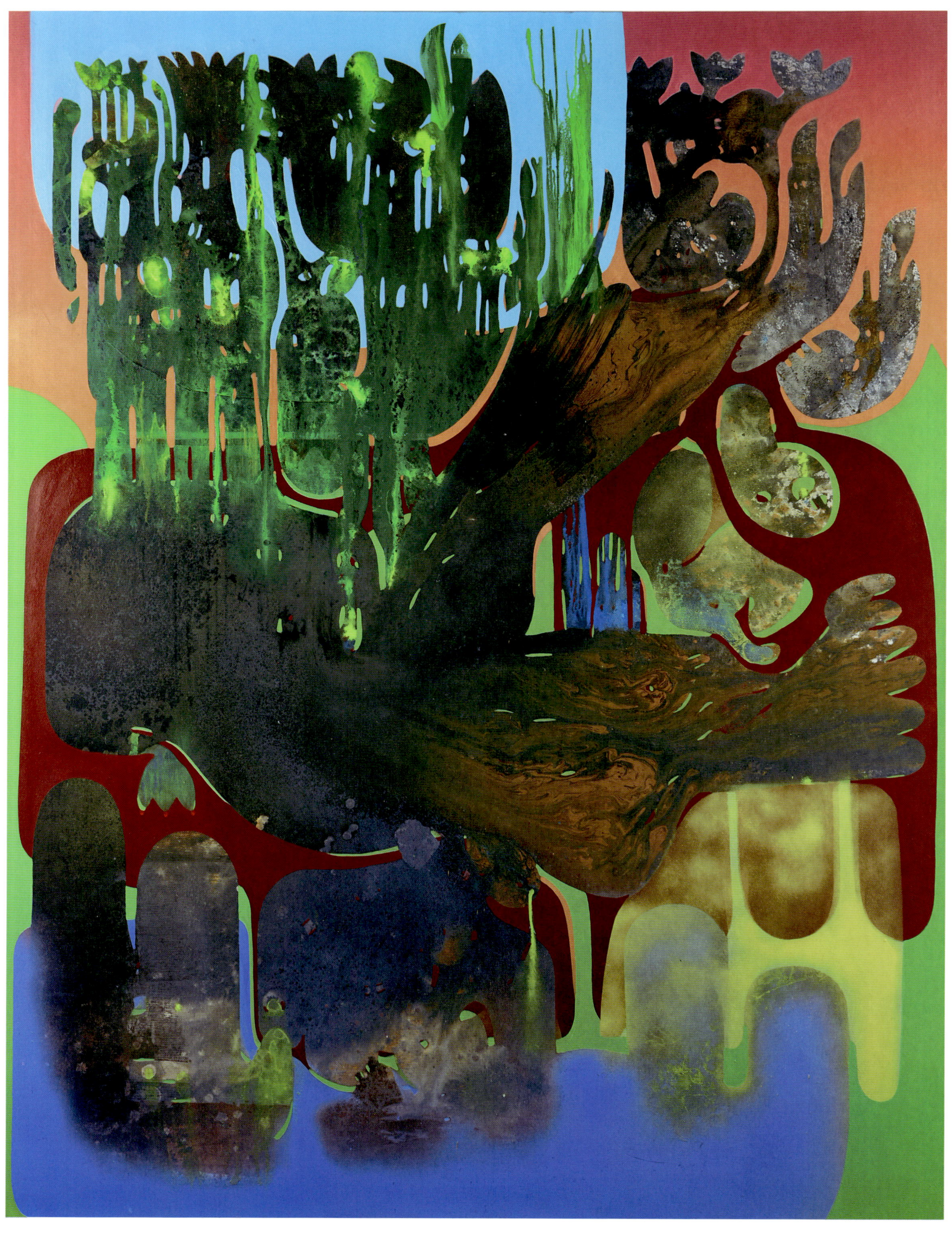

*Hanging Garde*n, 2022
Oil, acrylic, and pigment on canvas, 70 in. × 55 in. (177.8 cm × 139.7 cm)

Morphing, 2023
Oil, acrylic, and pigment on canvas, 72 in. × 67 in. (183 cm × 170.2 cm)

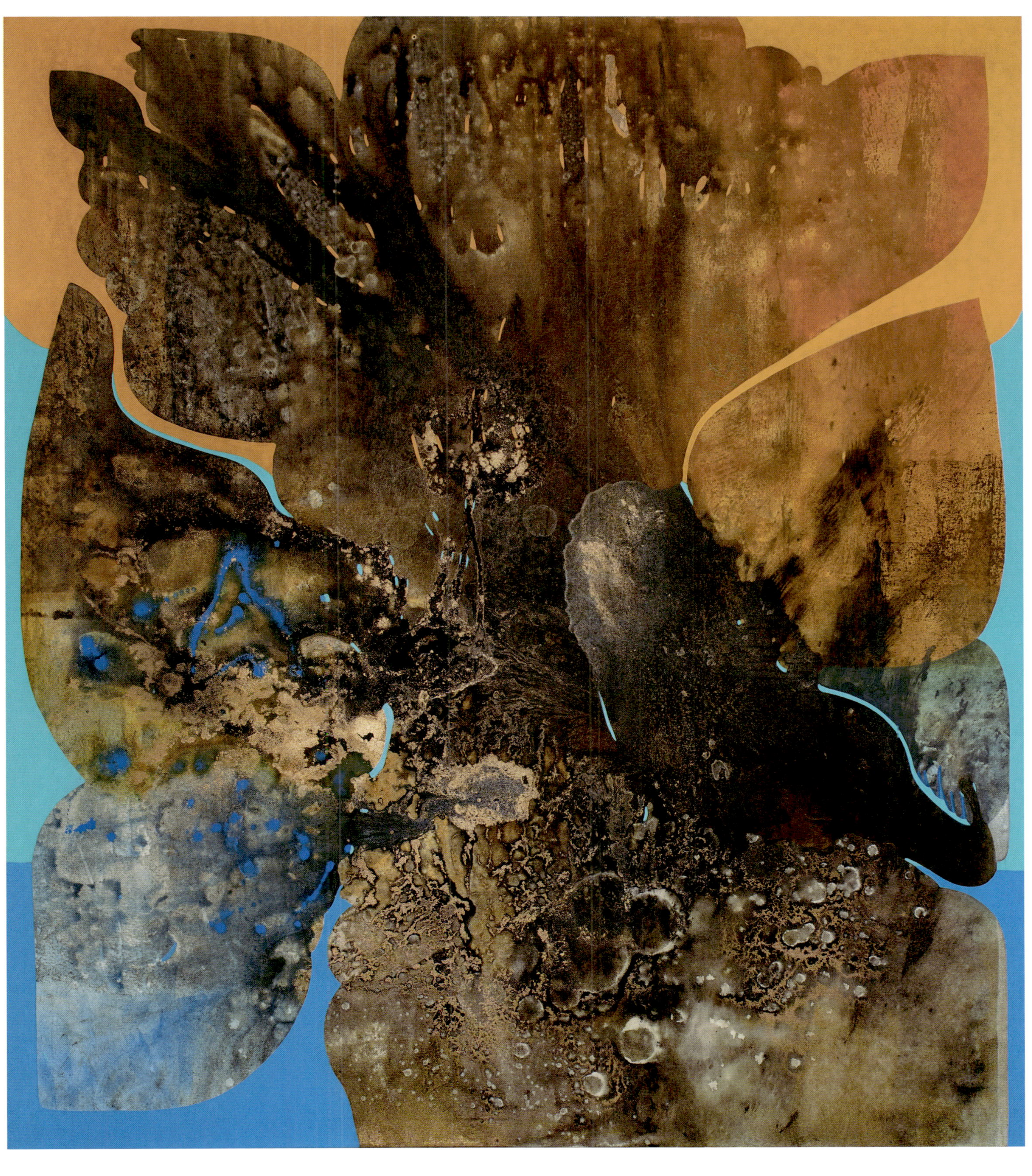

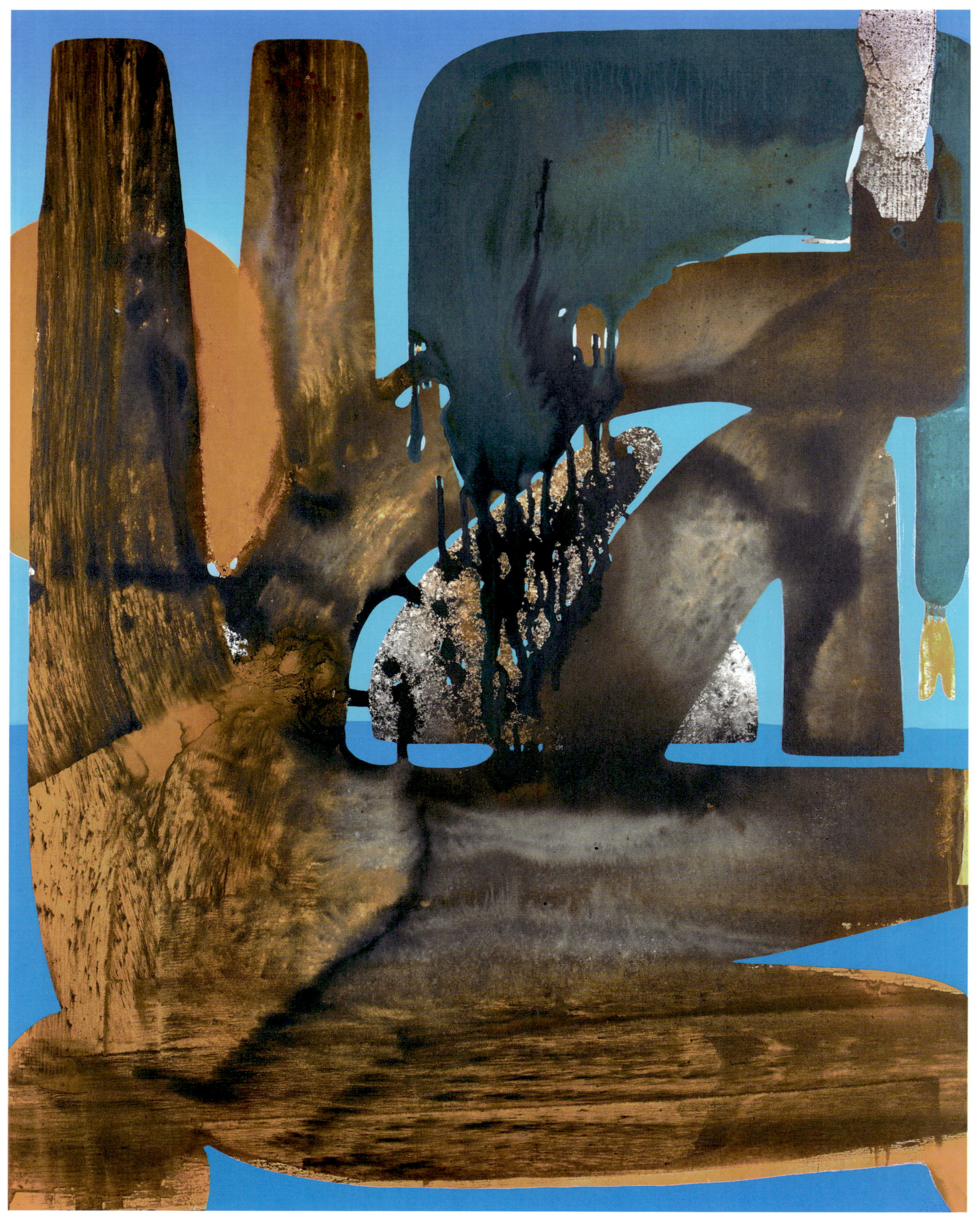

Outerworld II, 2021
Oil, acrylic, and pigment on canvas, 60 in. × 48 in. (152.4 cm × 122 cm)

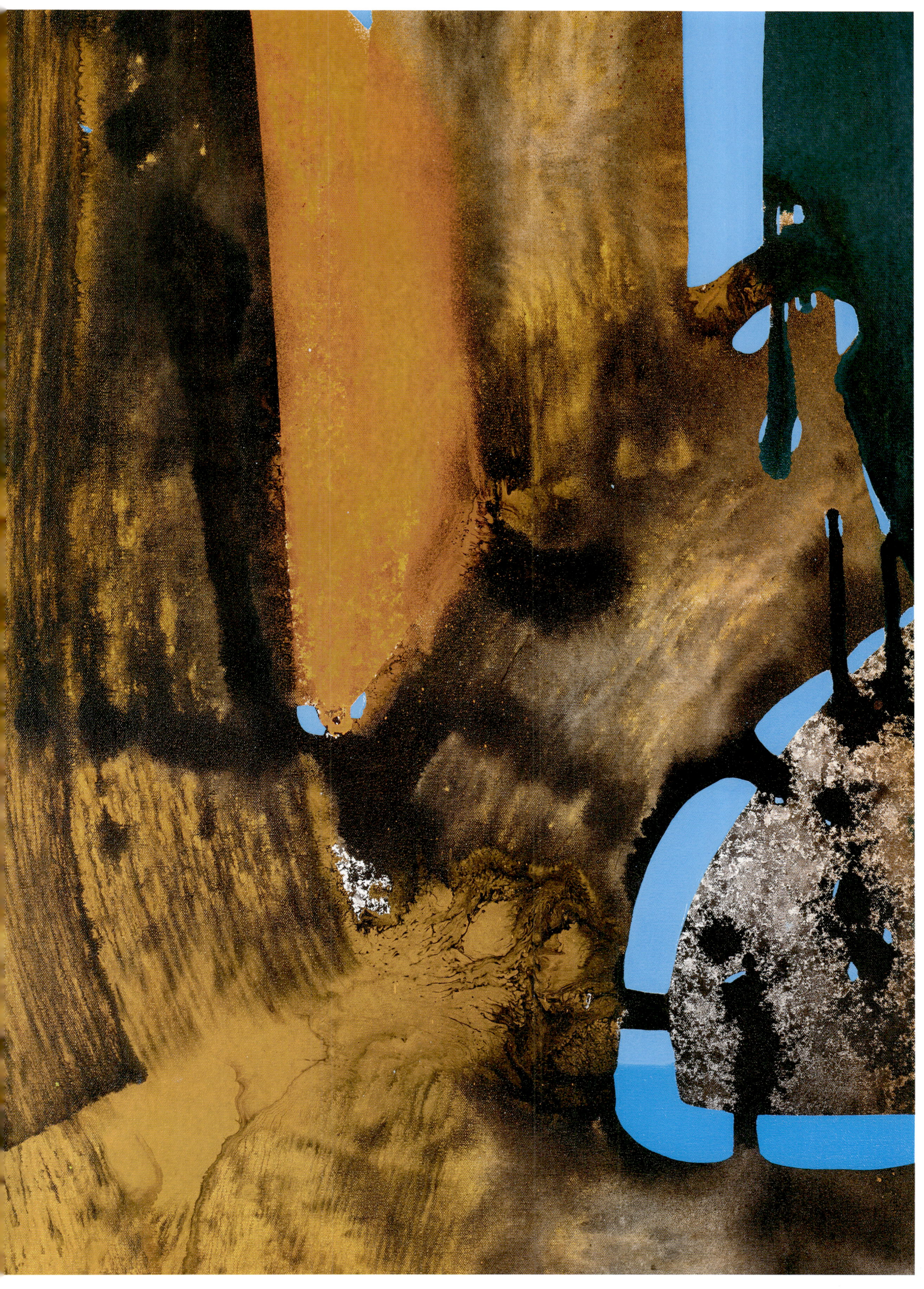

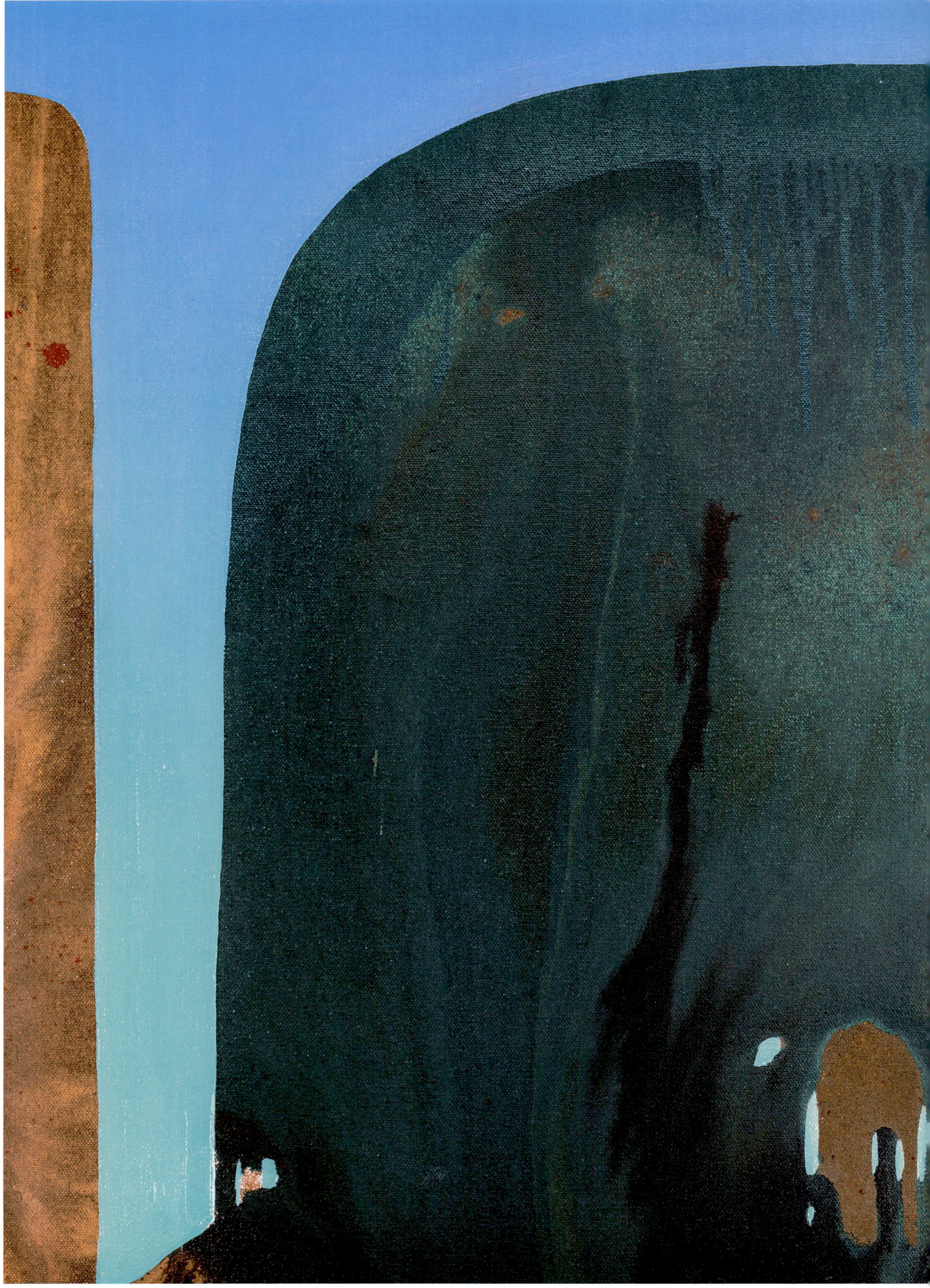

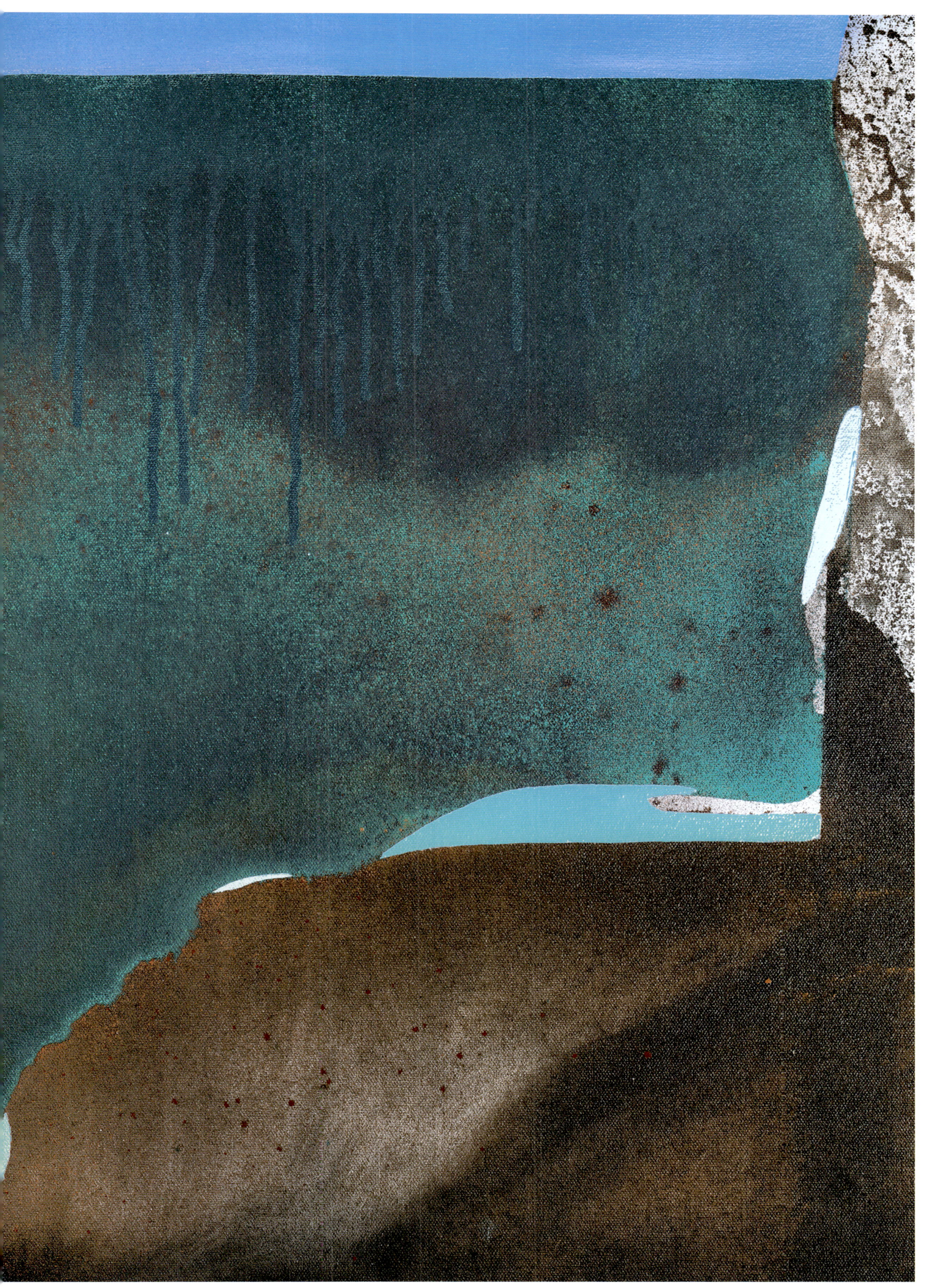

Additional Artworks

Other Worlds

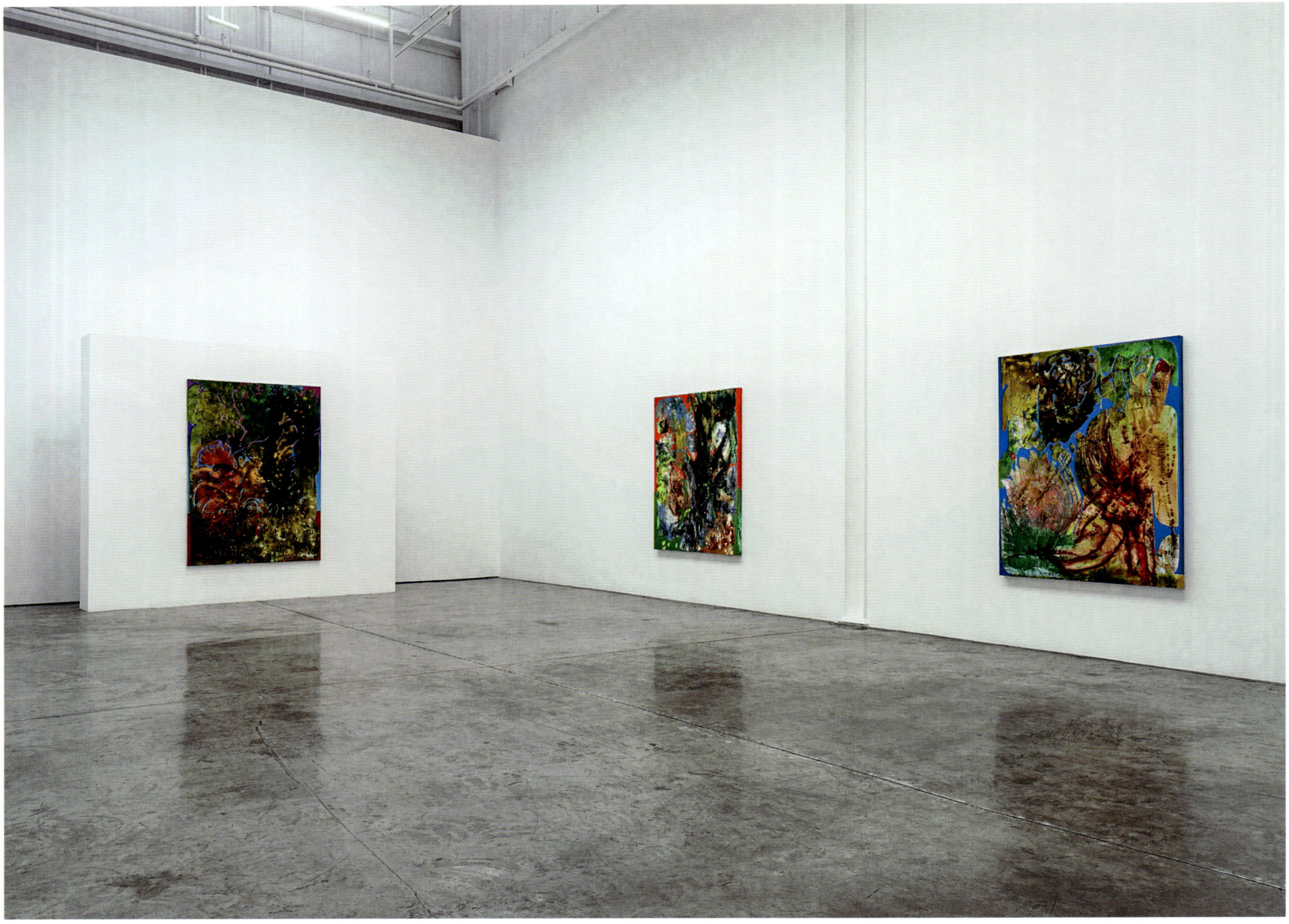

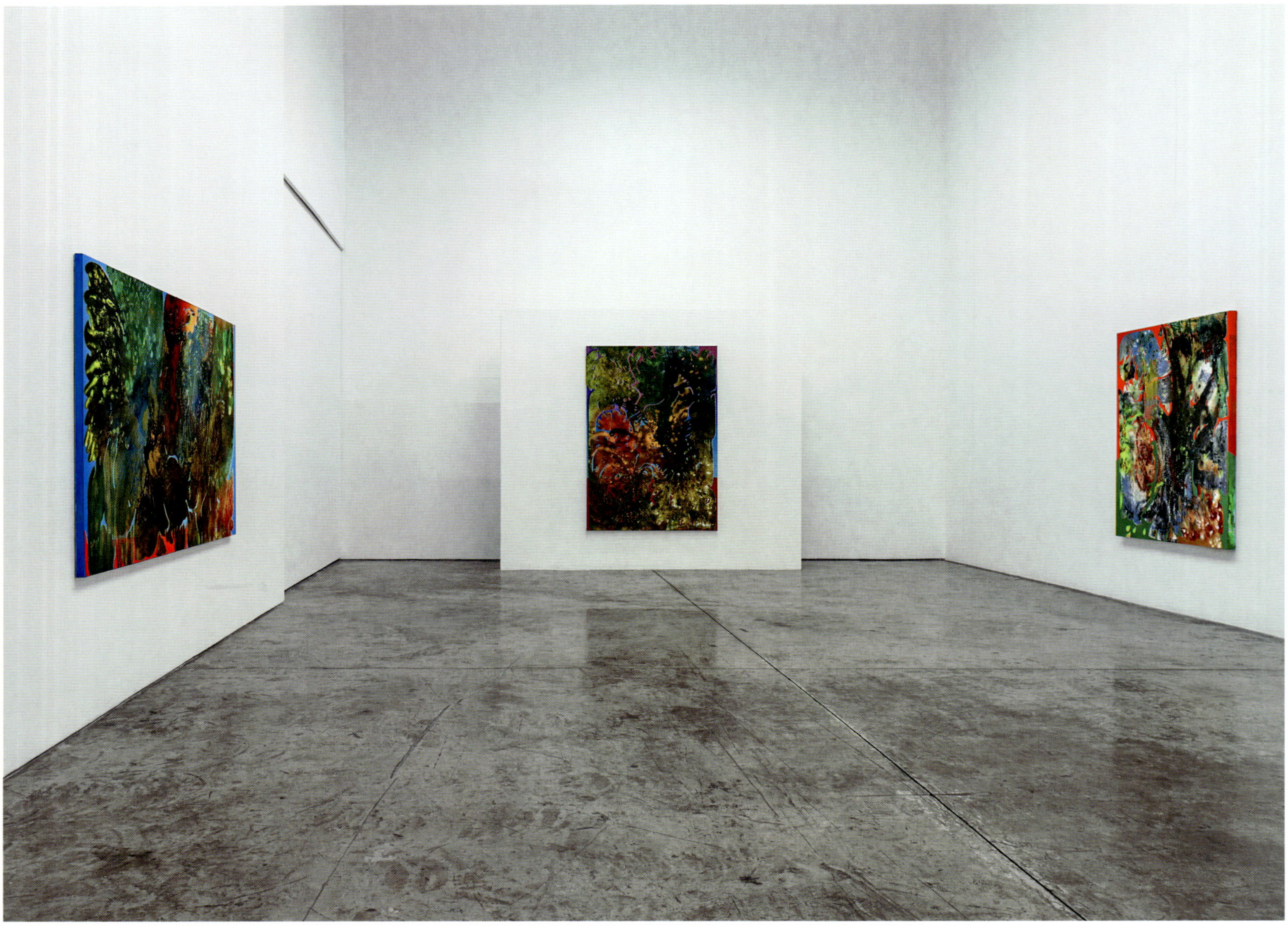

Installation view, *Vian Sora: House of Pearls*

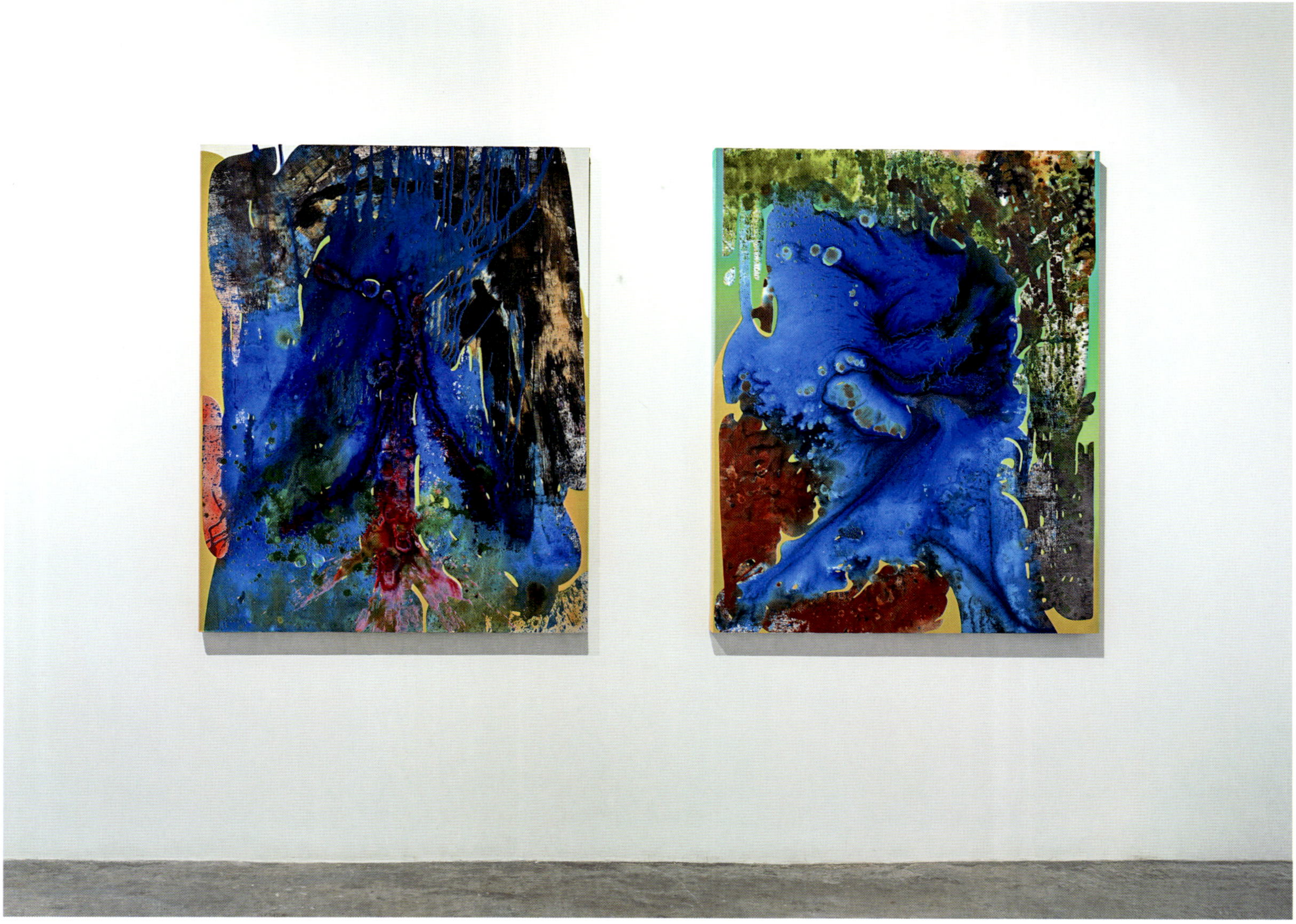

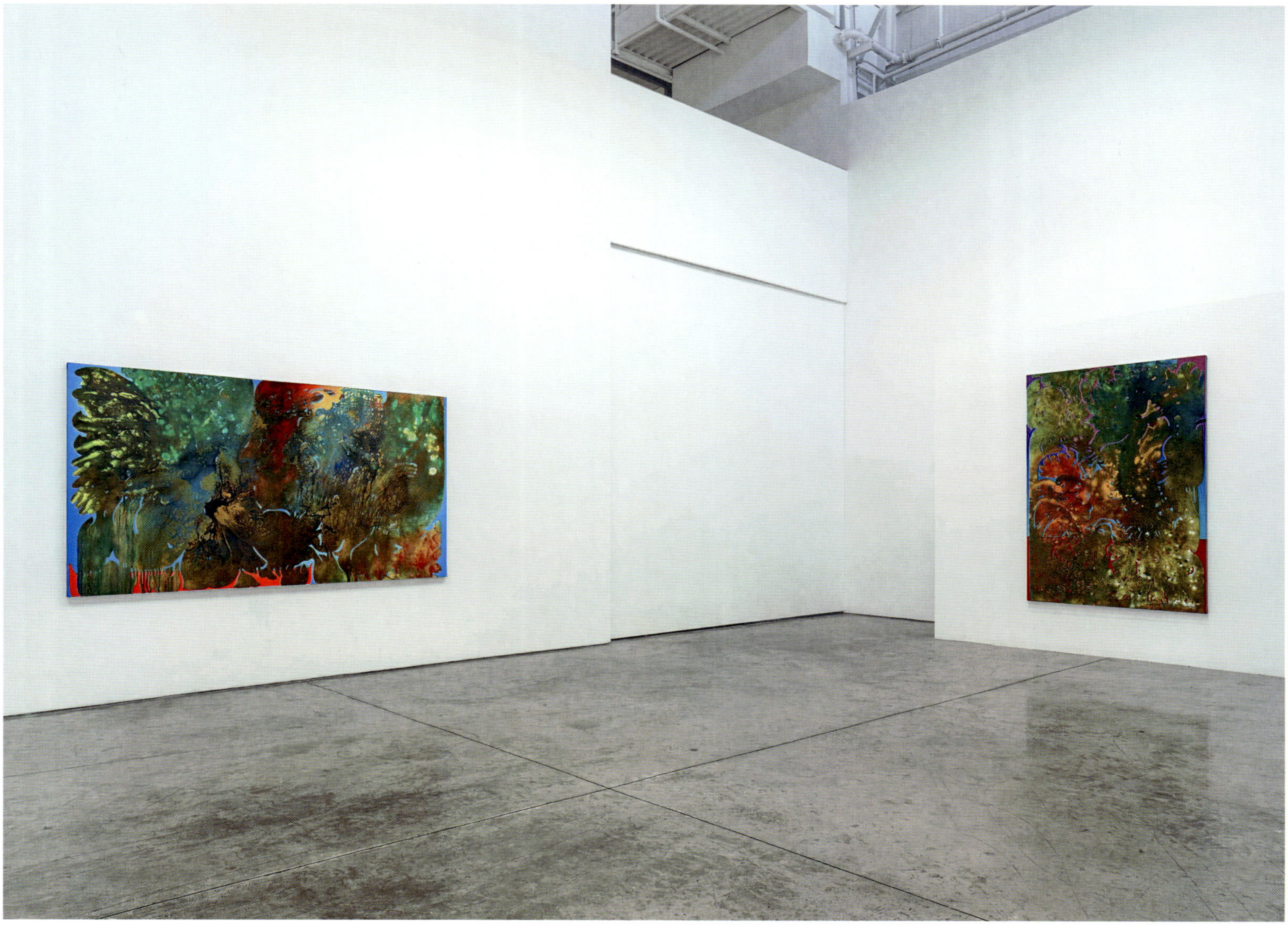

The Third Line, Dubai, October 31–December 10, 2024. Photos by Altamash Urooj

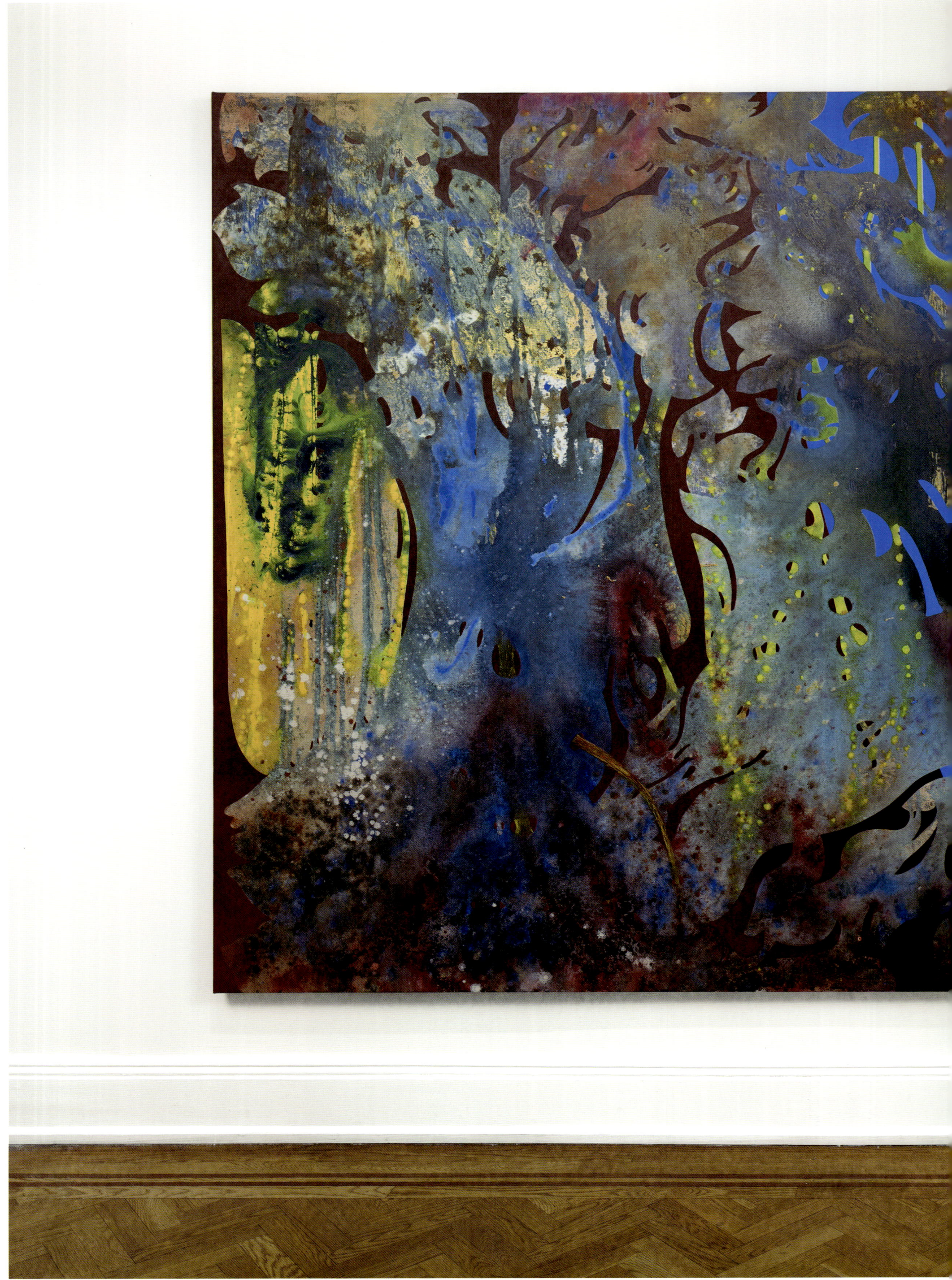

Dual Realms, 2024–25. Oil, acrylic, and pigment on canvas, 91 in. × 150 in. (231.1 cm × 381 cm)

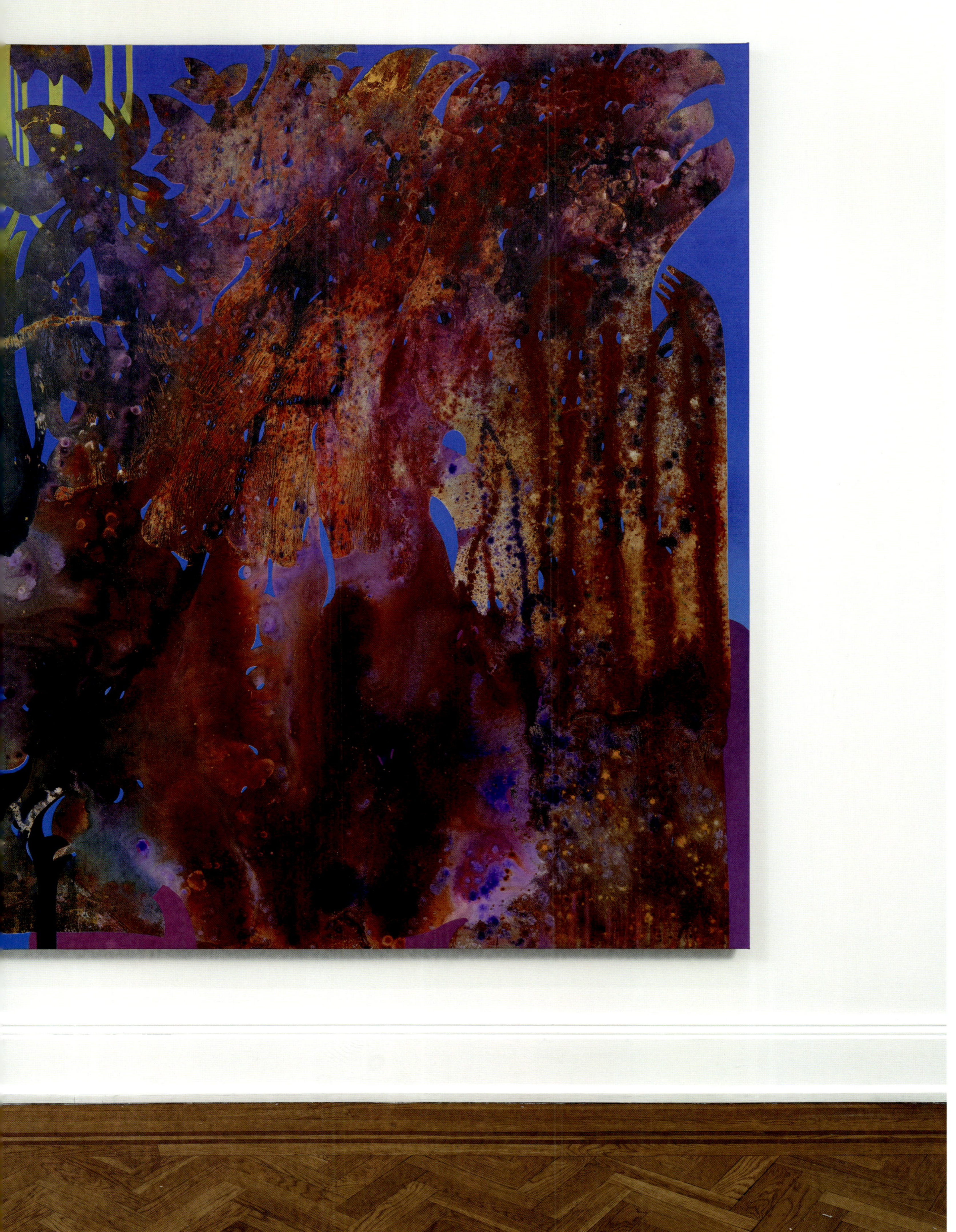

Exhale, 2024
Oil, acrylic, and pigment on canvas, 60 in. × 48 in. (152.4 cm × 122 cm)

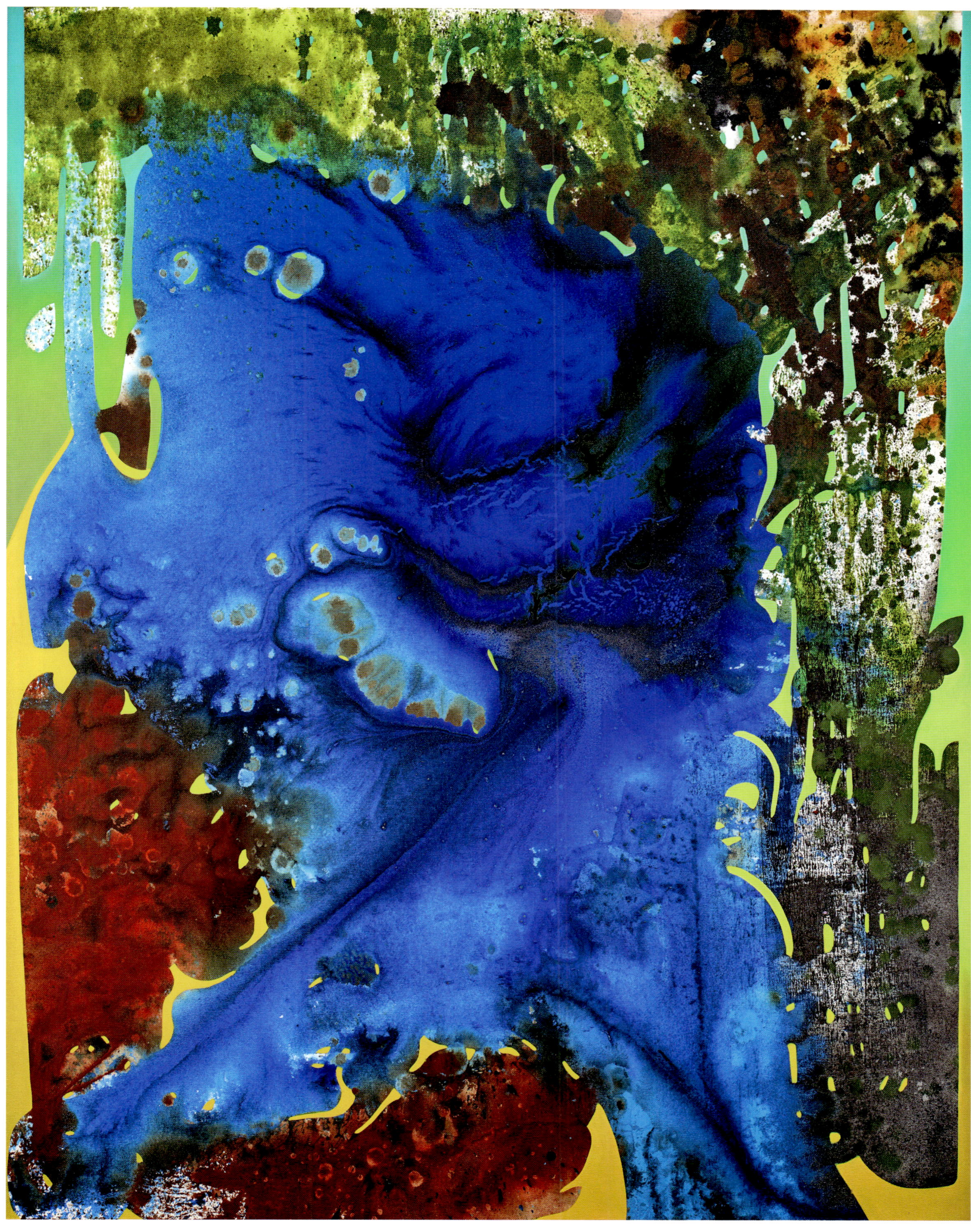

Inhale, 2024
Oil, acrylic, and pigment on canvas, 60 in. × 48 in. (152.4 cm × 122 cm)

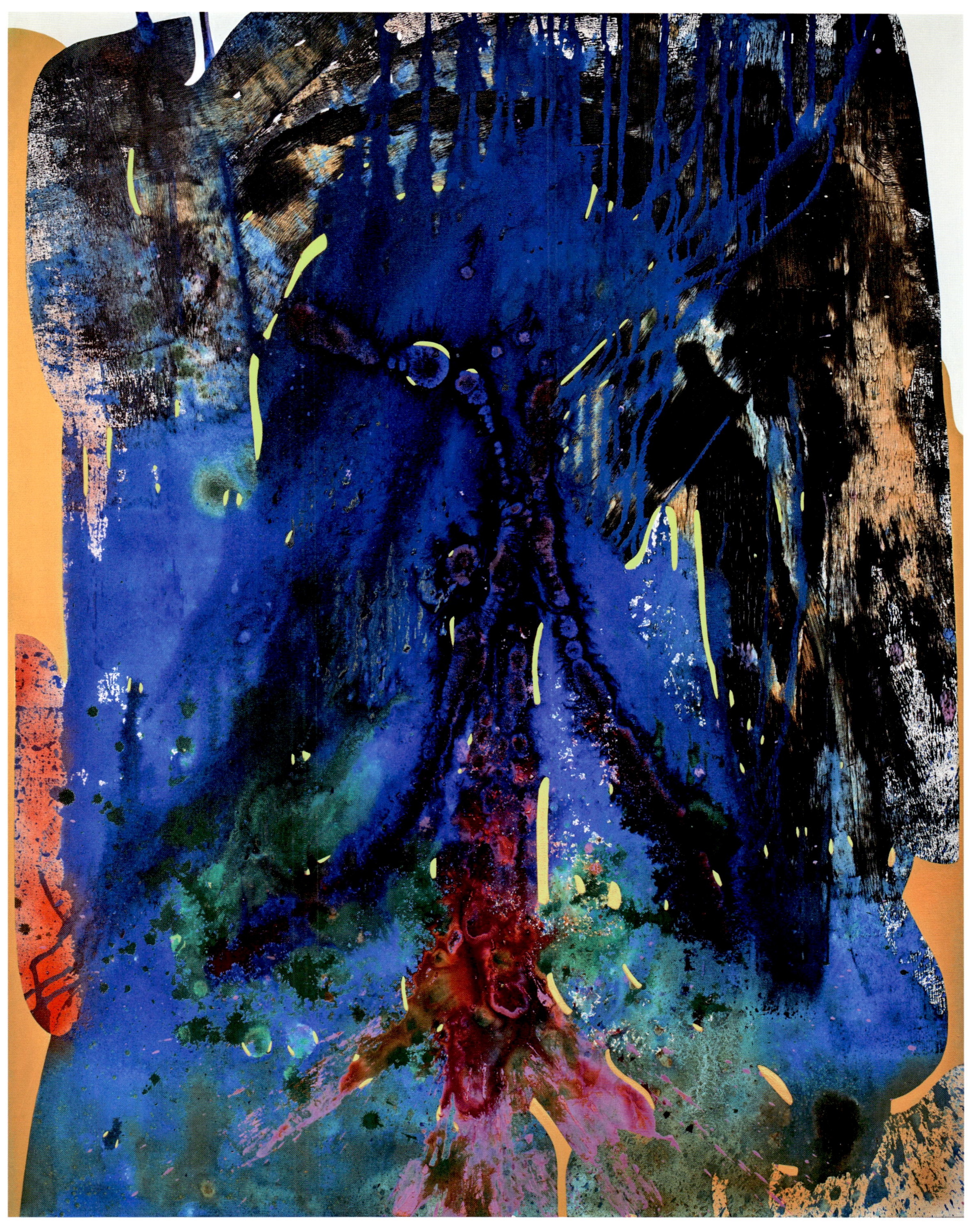

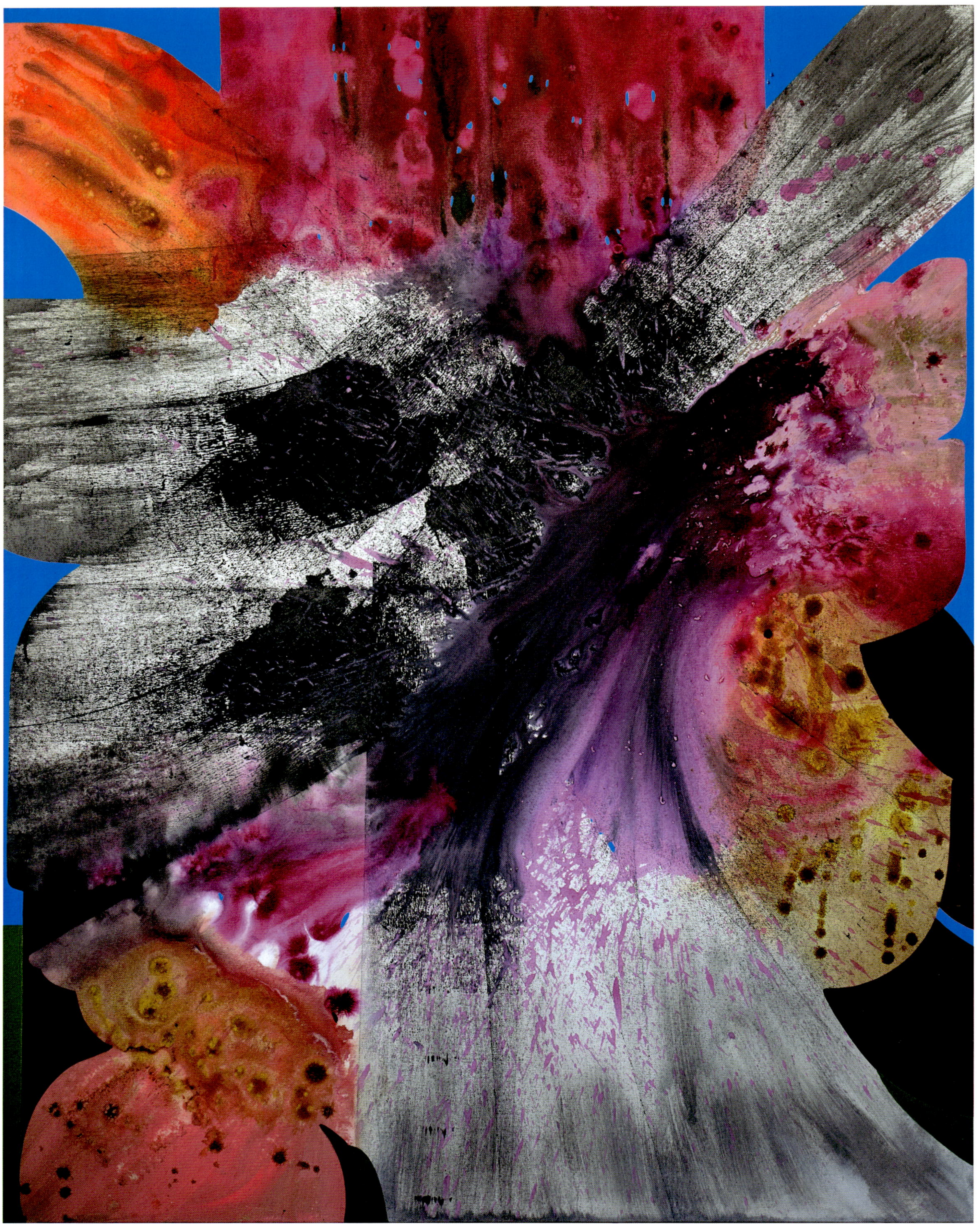

Umm Al-Binni, 2025
Oil, acrylic, and pigment on canvas, 60 in. × 48 in. (152.4 cm × 122 cm)

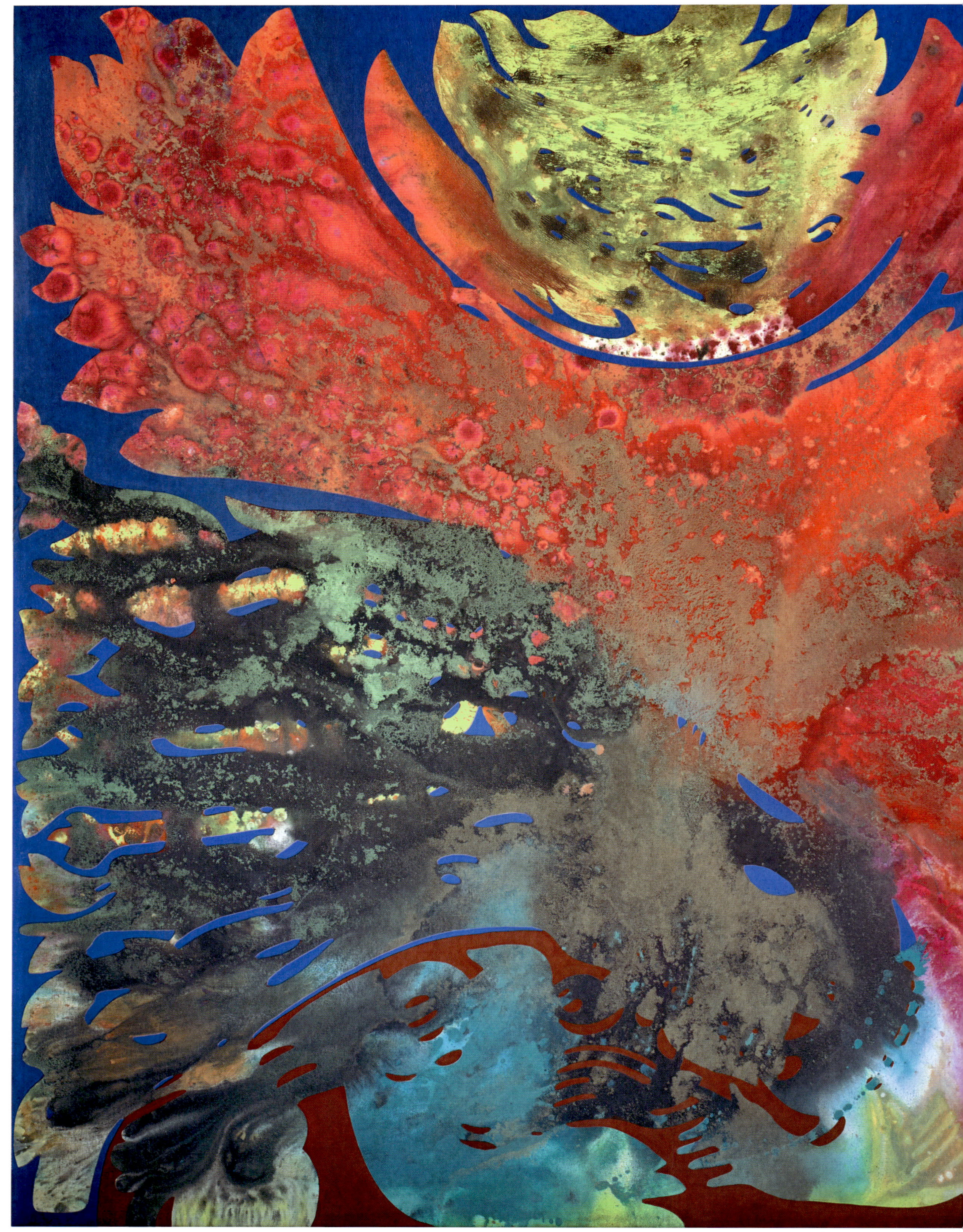

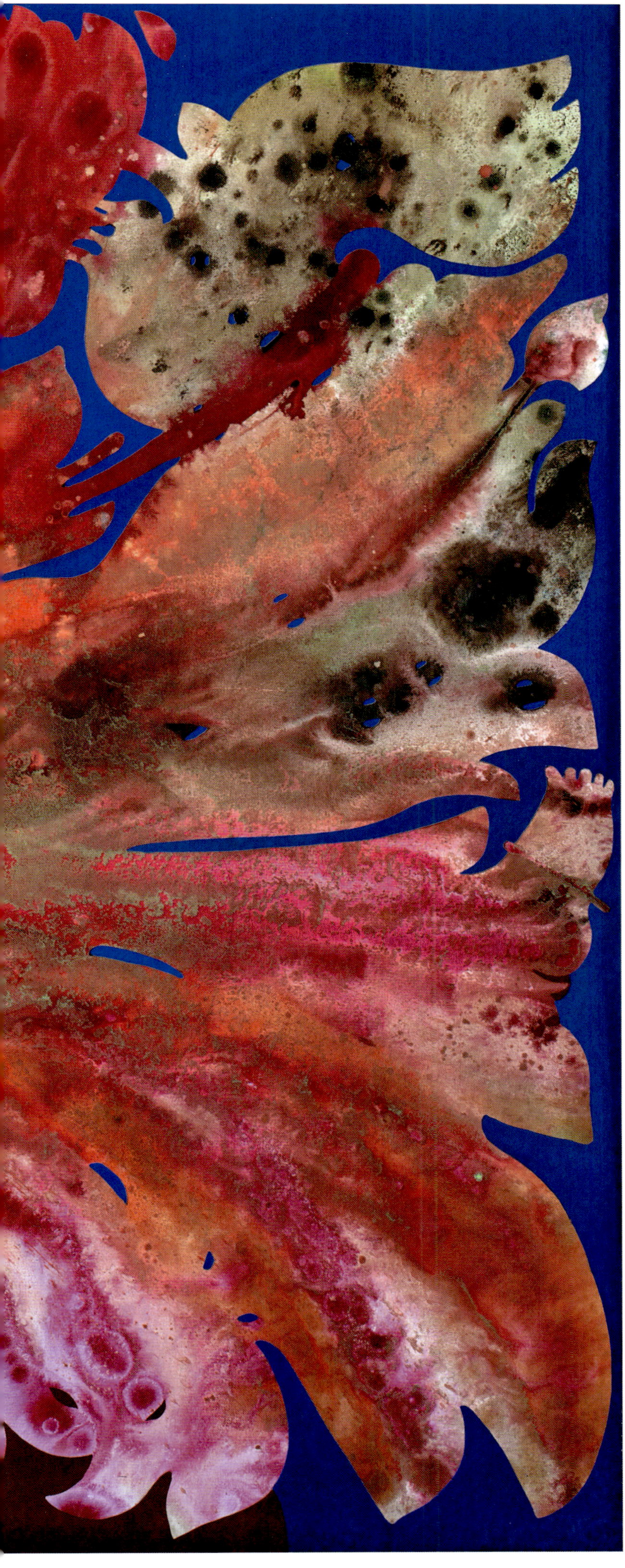

The Sky from Below, 2024–25
Oil, acrylic, and pigment on canvas, 75 in. × 90 in. (190.5 cm × 228.6 cm)

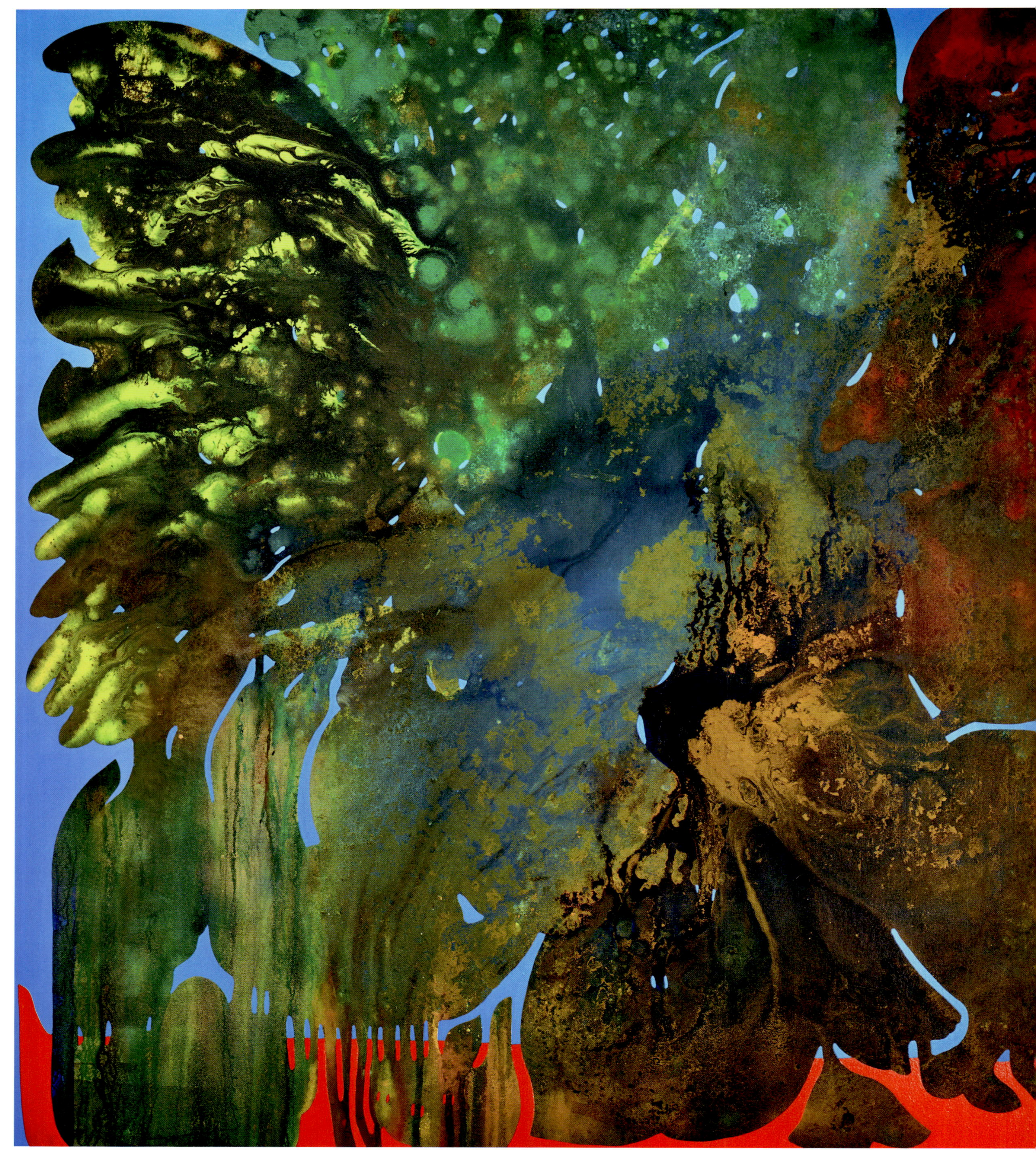

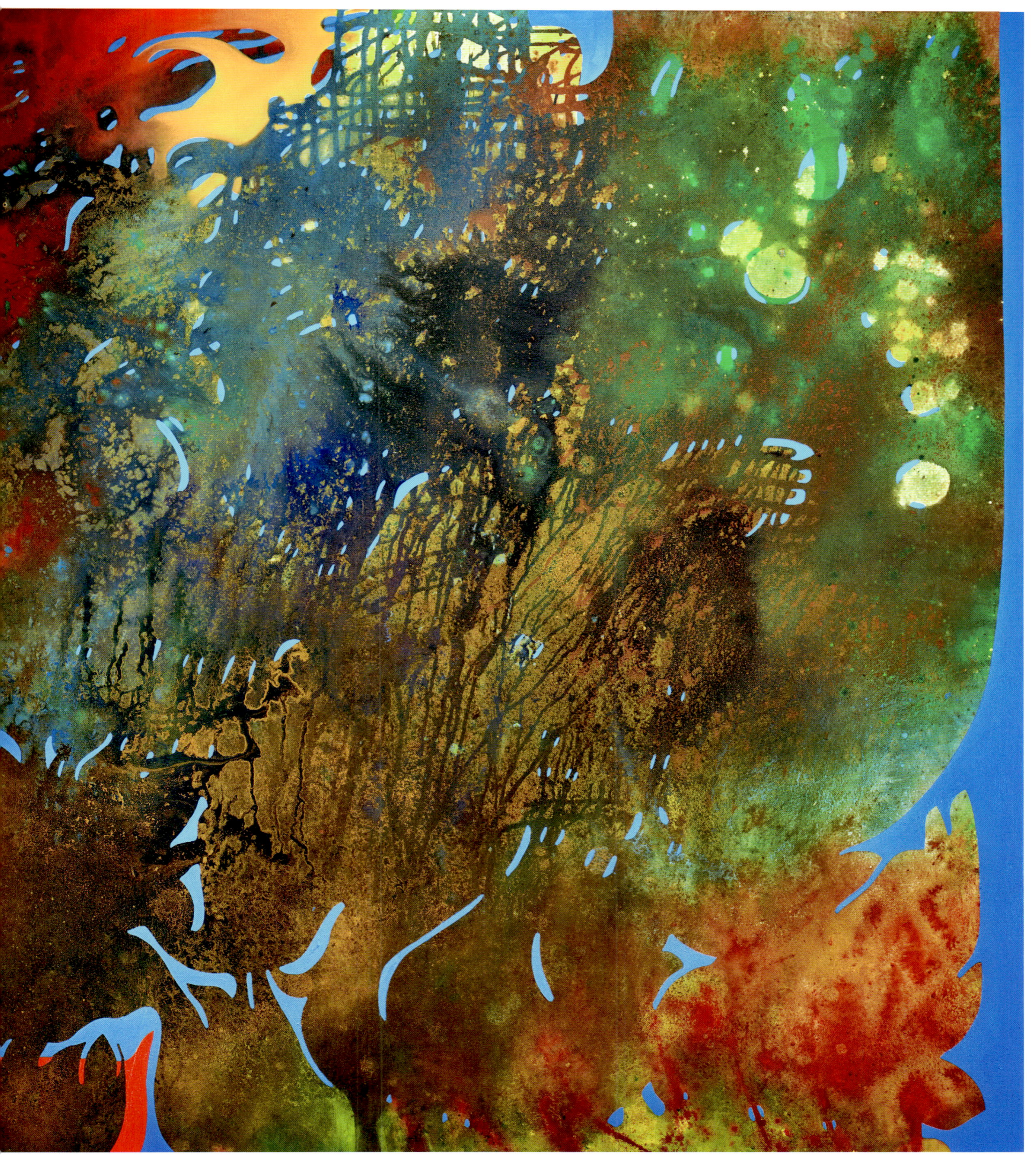

Previous page

Olivine, 2024.
Oil, acrylic, and pigment on canvas, 60 in. × 120 in. (152.4 cm × 304.8 cm)

On Art and Practice: Vian Sora and Tyler Blackwell

TB When did you first know painting was your thing? Was there a specific moment when it all just clicked for you?

VS Honestly, I think it was always going to happen. I grew up surrounded by artists and creatives, so it felt inevitable. But professionally, that moment came when I was nineteen and had my first group exhibition in Baghdad. Even before that, though, I remember receiving a book on technique by Vasari and meeting Faeq Hassan—those were huge for me. The discussions with Hassan and other Al-Ruwad artists, the instinct to express myself, the smells of a studio—those things all kept pulling me back to painting.

TB You met Faeq Hassan? What was he like?

VS I first met him as a child, then again before the Gulf War, and one last time in Paris a few years before he passed. I was about thirteen then, thirsty for knowledge. I remember being told to get my portfolio ready—he was visiting our family's auction house. I walked up to him with my uncle, carrying this big stack of drawings I had made that summer. He had this sharp gaze, these distinctive hands. Holding his pipe in one hand, he flipped through my work with the other and said that if I went to art school, it would ruin the innovation in my paintings. And I took that advice literally!

Later, after the Gulf War, I learned of his passing and found myself tracing every possible work he ever made. His lines were burned into my memory.

TB You were around art a lot, it seems. Your family used to run an auction house in Baghdad, right? What do you remember about it?

VS It was a proper auction house and antiques market in the city. There were regular auctions where people—artists, locals, expats—would come out to gather and enjoy community like it was a gallery opening. It was a sort of public salon that brought together friends, family, kids, and dreamers (like me), and very serious, interesting people like Hassan.

TB Besides Hassan, who else has influenced your work?

VS So many. Off the top of my head—Willem de Kooning, Chaim Soutine, Francis Bacon, Rafa Al-Nasiri, Shakir Hassan Al Said, Albert Oehlen, Cecily Brown, Anselm Kiefer, Max Ernst, Etel Adnan, Rita Ackermann, Jawad Salim, Louise Bourgeois, Zaha Hadid, Baya, Joan Mitchell, Charline von Heyl, Dana Schutz, Marlene Dumas ...

TB Do you miss Baghdad?

VS Every second. It's the one city I can't find anywhere else. I spent my first twenty-nine years there, and it still exists in me. I dream about it all the time—Al-Mutanabbi Street, the banks of the Tigris, the Abbasid-era architecture, the endless palm trees. But the real essence of Baghdad is how it carries its wounds, how it rebuilds itself over and over.

I still vividly remember my studio there, with that massive palm tree outside the balcony, and my

Fig. 8

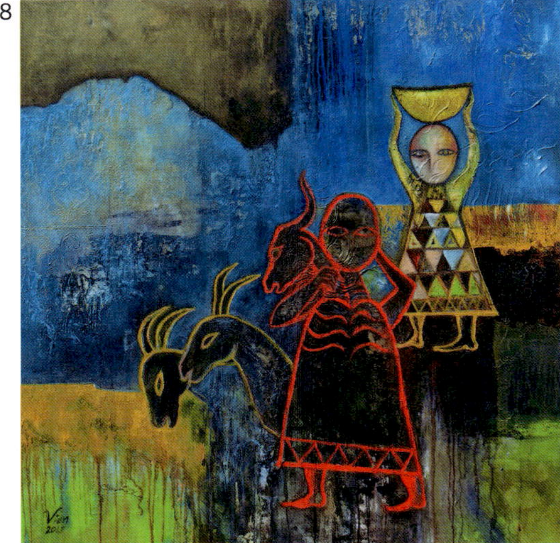

Vian Sora, *A Place to Get Lost*, 2016.
Oil, acrylic, and pigment on canvas,
48 in. × 48 in. (122 cm × 122 cm). Courtesy the artist.

Fig. 7

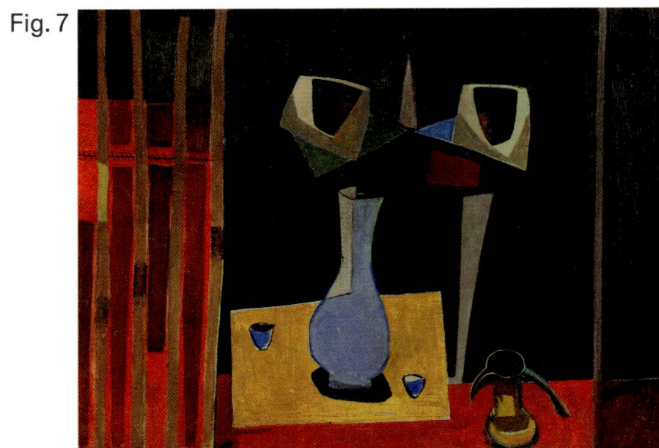

Faeq Hassan (Iraqi, 1914–1992), *Bedouin Tent*, 1950.
Oil on wood, 22.8 in. × 29 in. (57.9 cm × 73.7 cm).
Courtesy Barjeel Art Foundation, Sharjah.

grandparents' house, full of hidden corners and gardens. Those places are still alive in my mind.

TB Speaking of the studio, these days you spend so much time there—sometimes fifteen, sixteen hours straight. I'd go cross-eyed. Do you have any creative rituals to keep you going?

VS Yeah, I'm in there an average of twelve hours a day, sometimes more if deadlines are looming. The longer I'm there, the more I get into the zone. There's no bargaining with the canvas—it's endurance, patience, repetition. I stretch and meditate daily, walk and swim when I can, and practice tai chi most mornings. But full transparency, I could be better about taking care of my body.

TB And sleep? I know you've struggled with that. We have commiserated over rest.

VS Oh yeah, I barely sleep. I know it's the PTSD—growing up in Baghdad during real war meant sleeping with one eye open. That never really went away. I still experience lucid dreams, hallucinations, sleep paralysis. My mind blurs the line between reality and dreams, and that seeps into my work.

But it's not all dark—sometimes I experience places of immense beauty and joy that I can't explain. Those visions find their way into my paintings too.

TB How do those images translate into your work?

VS Memory is everything to my process. I'm fascinated by how the brain processes and interprets imagery—how certain symbols or compositions activate personal or cultural associations. My work tries to weave together personal and collective memories, blending ancient Mesopotamian motifs with abstract painting traditions. It's a way of morphing dark experiences into brightness, of learning how to balance chaos with harmony.

TB That makes sense—your work always feels like it's hovering between abstraction and something just almost recognizable. When you start something new, how do you decide where to go with it?

VS I think it's a mix of memory, subconscious imagery, and current events. My process is layered, literally and metaphorically. I start with drawings, then lay the canvas flat on the floor and apply color rapidly. After 2015, I started working with explosion scenes—reversing and transforming them into new scenarios. Months can pass with me adding and stripping paint. It's a constant negotiation—between me, the work, my memories, my ideas, my colors, my tools.

TB Do you think your work helps preserve history?

VS Yes. Painting can be a time capsule. Without cave paintings, ancient sculptures, or artifacts, we wouldn't understand past civilizations. And in times of war, artists preserve the stories that often get erased. We remember what others might try to forget.

TB Which brings us to *Outerworlds*—the title of our show. We've talked about how this word suggests

Fig. 9

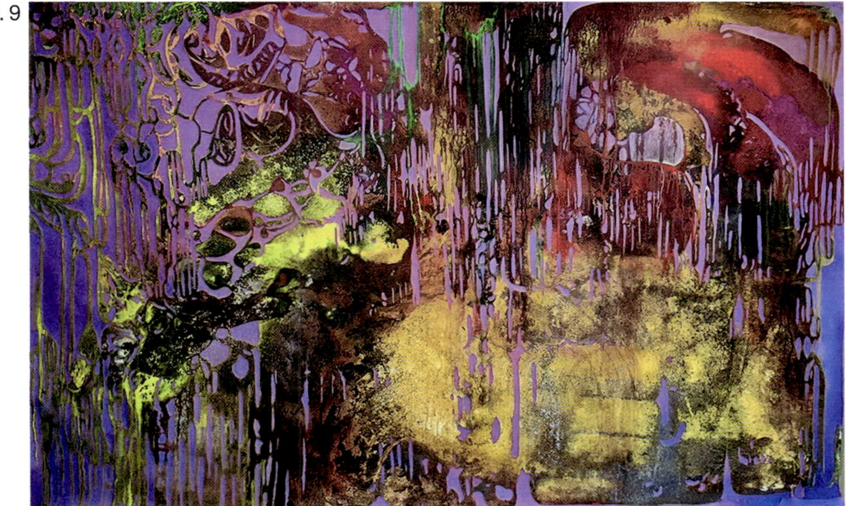

Vian Sora, *Vespertine*, 2017. Oil, acrylic, and pigment on Arches paper, 54 in. × 85 in. (137 cm × 216 cm). Courtesy the artist.

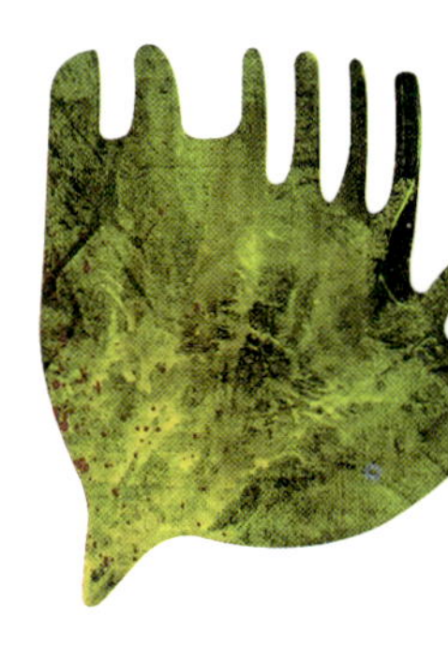

some kind of "other" landscape. How do you approach landscapes in your work?

VS I think of my landscapes as existing outside of a single place. They're abstract, built through unexpected colors and shapes that don't tether them to reality. I use intense, often unnatural color combinations to push beyond traditional representation and evoke emotion instead.

TB And color itself—do you think certain colors express certain emotions?

VS Absolutely. Texture too. Scraped, multilayered surfaces create depth and history, while drips or splatters capture chaos or spontaneity. I take my time preparing colors—using highly pigmented paints and slow-drying techniques. Some hues reflect my environment, but I like to disrupt them with unexpected contrasts, mirroring what's happening in my life or the world.

TB Do you see your paintings as a conversation with the viewer?

VS A silent one, perhaps, yes. I want people to engage with my work in their own way, bringing their emotions and interpretations. I don't dictate the meaning—I just invite the journey. I'm interested in breaking boundaries and crossing borders (in life and in your mind!), but I have no interest in determining what the viewer might take away from the work.

TB That openness makes your work feel vulnerable in a way, too, then. Do you feel vulnerable while painting?

VS Sometimes. People often want to reduce my work to war, tragedy, personal loss—which, yes, are part of it. But I also have a sense of humor! I live a pretty whimsical life in many ways, and that has helped me process my history. I like to honor the joy of playfulness and community in my work too. We are all layered beings.

TB Ok, the ultimate interview question—how do you know when a painting is finished?

VS When there's nothing left to solve. I avoid the idea of "perfect"—life isn't perfect, and memory isn't exact. A painting needs a certain tension, a moment where it still feels alive.

TB You've been in Louisville for sixteen years now. How has Kentucky influenced your work?

VS Louisville has a deeply creative, artistic energy—it's actually both global and local. The storytelling culture and craft traditions also connect with my Iraqi and Kurdish heritage in ways I didn't expect.

TB Do you think that folks from the Gulf region experience your paintings differently than Americans do?

VS Yes, I think there is a sense of familiarity for many, but also every subculture in the Gulf and broader Middle East experiences the paintings differently. For many people, the imagery is surprising because the paintings try to upend expected patterns and perception/cultural boundaries are broken. But then there is also familiar, ancient iconography that is at the foundation of my work. I like to think

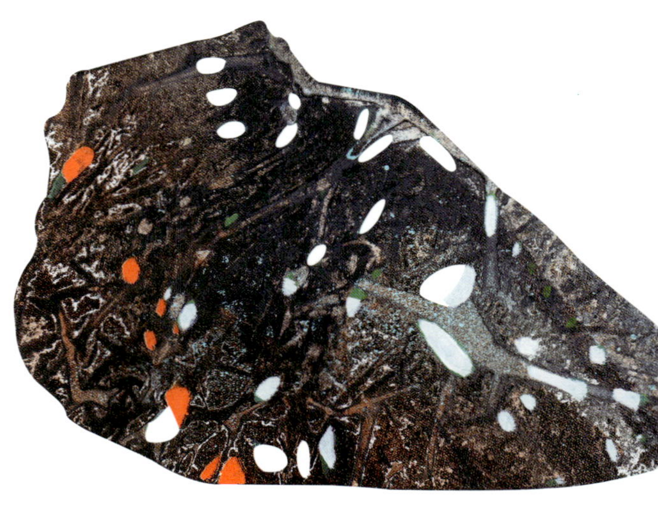

this sort of imagery points to a broader, collective understanding.

TB And if someone walks away from your exhibition feeling just one thing, what do you hope it is?

VS A sense of connection.

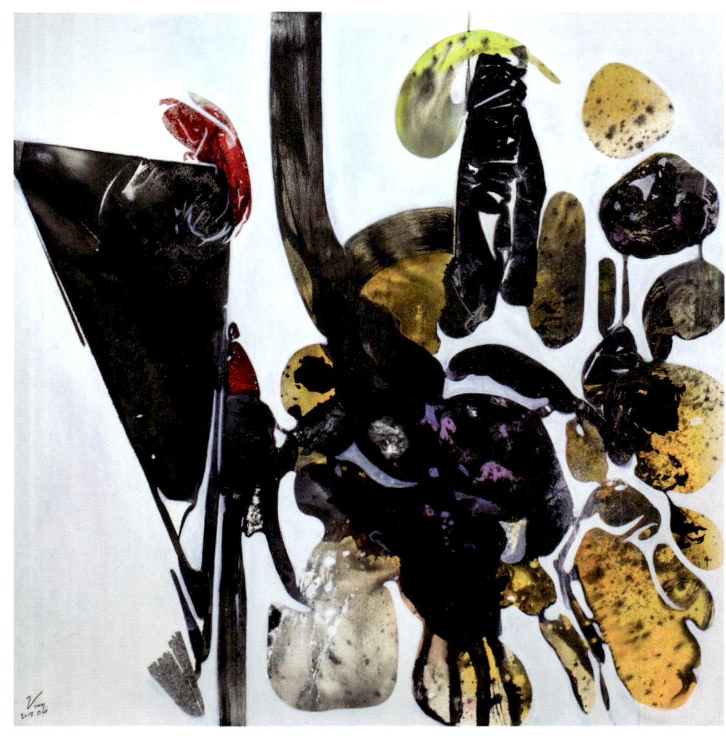

Landscape with a Moth, 2016
Acrylic on canvas, 48 in. × 48 in. (122 cm × 122 cm)
Courtesy of Judson and Daphne Hartlage

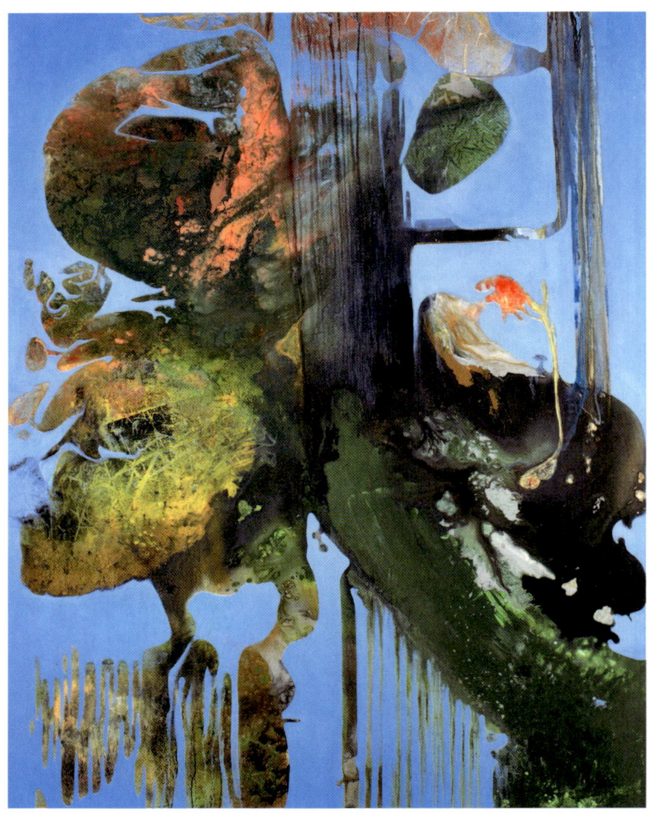

Earth Lines, 2016
Acrylic finished with oil on canvas, 60 in. × 48 in. (154.2 cm × 122 cm)
Courtesy Erik Eaker

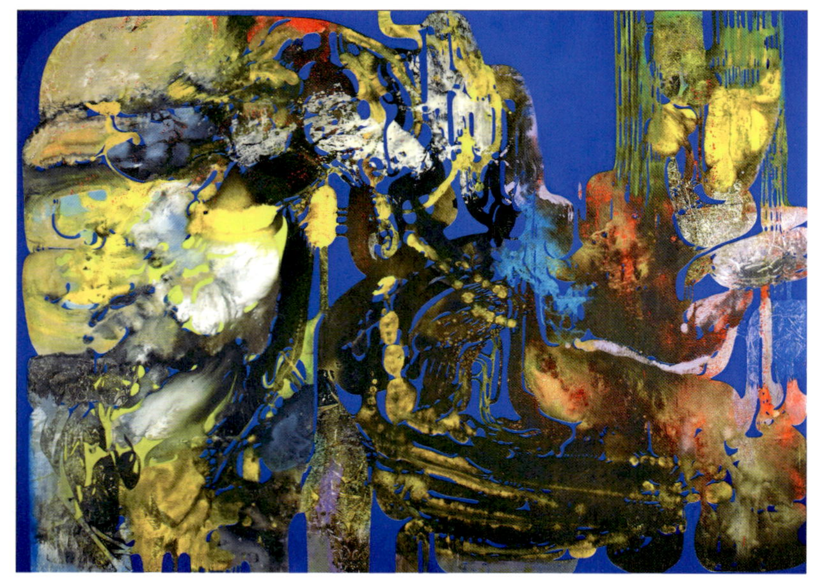

Echo and Narcissus, 2018
Oil, acrylic, and pigment on canvas, 84 in. × 60 in. (213.4 cm × 152.4 cm)
Speed Art Museum, Museum Purchase with funds
generously donated by Stephen Reily and Emily Bingham,
Reverend Alfred R. Shands III, Larry Shapin and
Ladonna Nicolas, and Erik Eaker and John Brooks

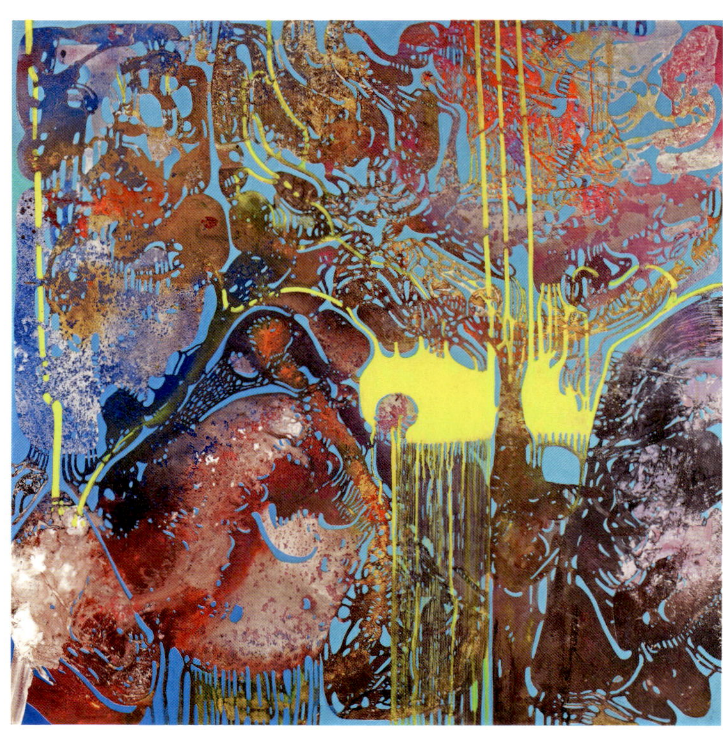

Citizen, 2019
Oil, acrylic, and pigment on canvas, 48 in. × 48 in. (122 cm × 122 cm)
Collection of Michael and Stephanie Morris

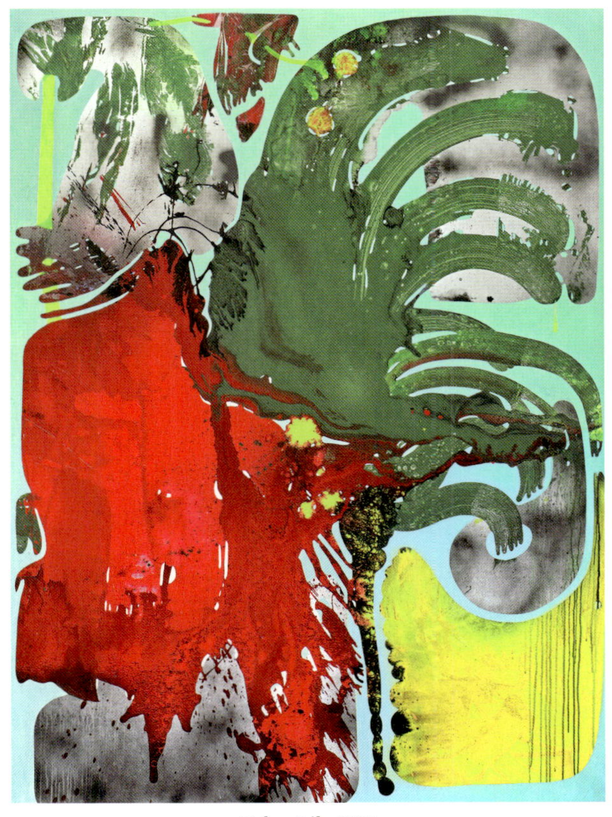

Cobra Lily, 2020
Oil, acrylic, and pigment on canvas, 79 in. × 59 in. (200.7 cm × 150 cm)
Collection of Drs. Kaveh and Heather Zamanian

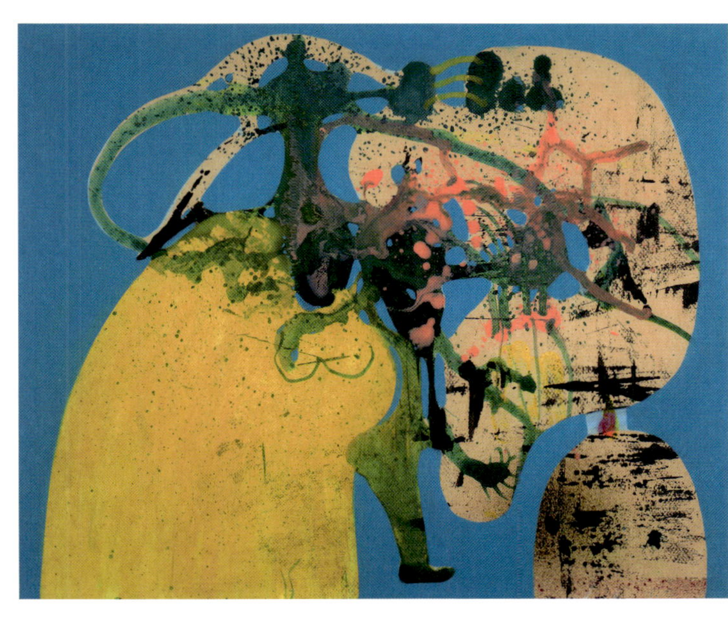

Antibodies, 2020
Acrylic on paper, 16 in. × 20 in. (40.6 cm × 50.8 cm)
Private collection

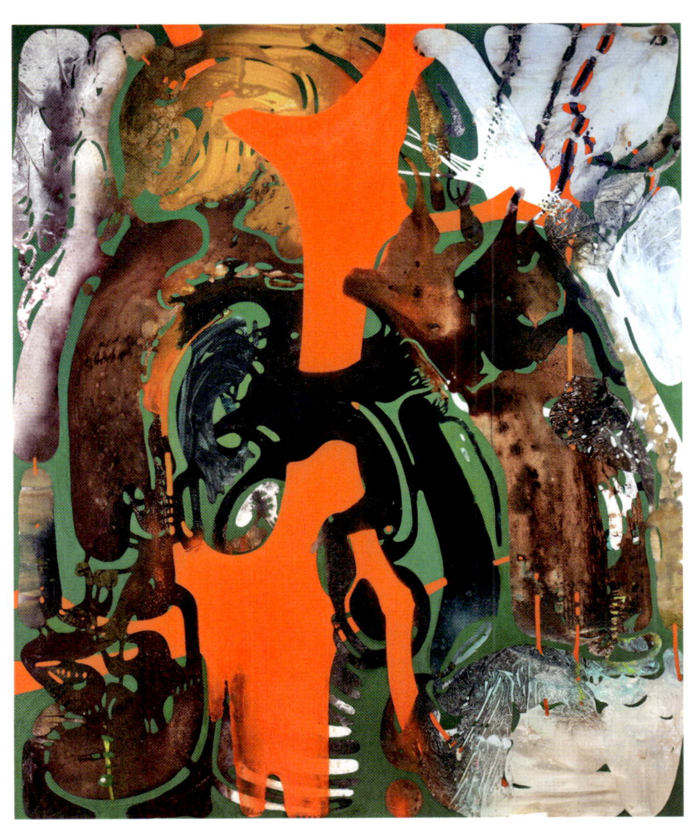

Woodlands, 2020
Oil, acrylic, and pigment on canvas, 72 in. × 60 in. (183 cm × 152.4 cm)
Speed Art Museum, Bequest of the Mary Norton Shands
and Alfred R. Shands III Art Collection

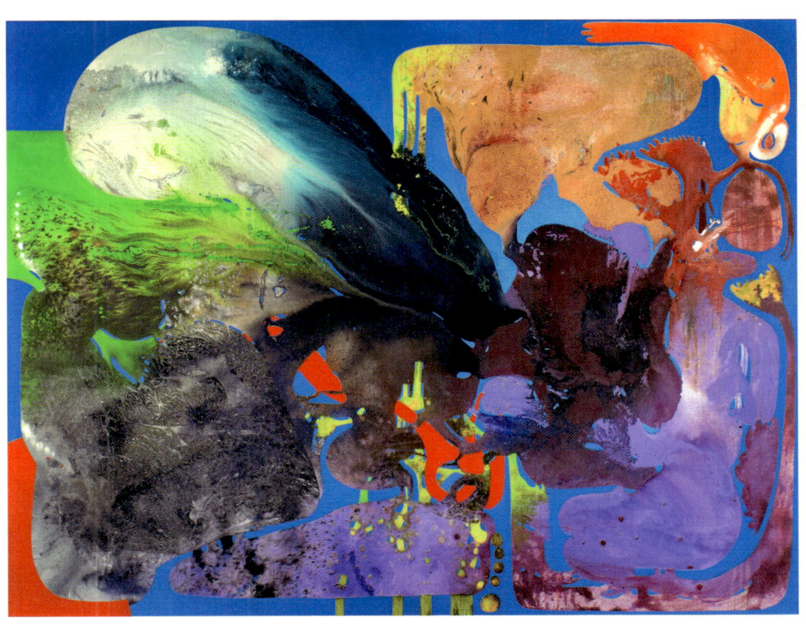

Floodgates, 2021
Oil, acrylic, and pigment on canvas, 72 in. × 96 in. (183 cm × 243.8 cm)
Courtesy Kentucky Performing Arts Foundation

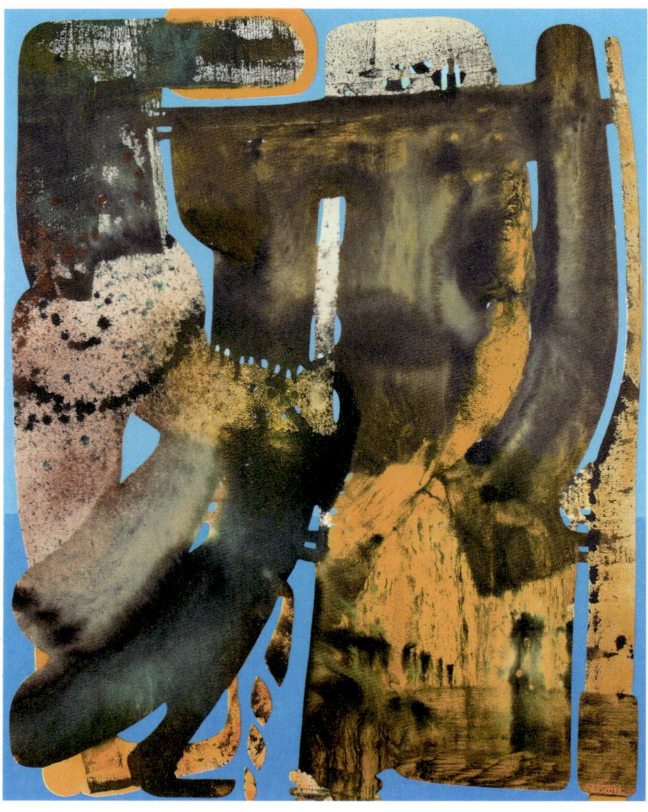

Outerworld I, 2021
Oil, acrylic, and pigment on canvas, 60 in. × 48 in. (152.4 cm × 122 cm)
Collection of Brook and Pam Smith

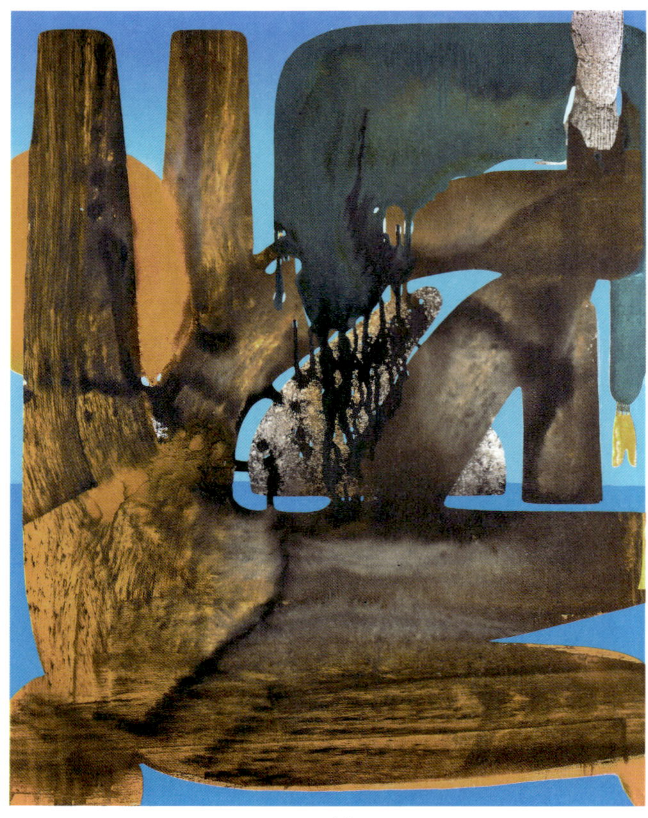

Outerworld II, 2021
Oil, acrylic, and pigment on canvas, 60 in. × 48 in. (152.4 cm × 122 cm)
Collection of Brook and Pam Smith

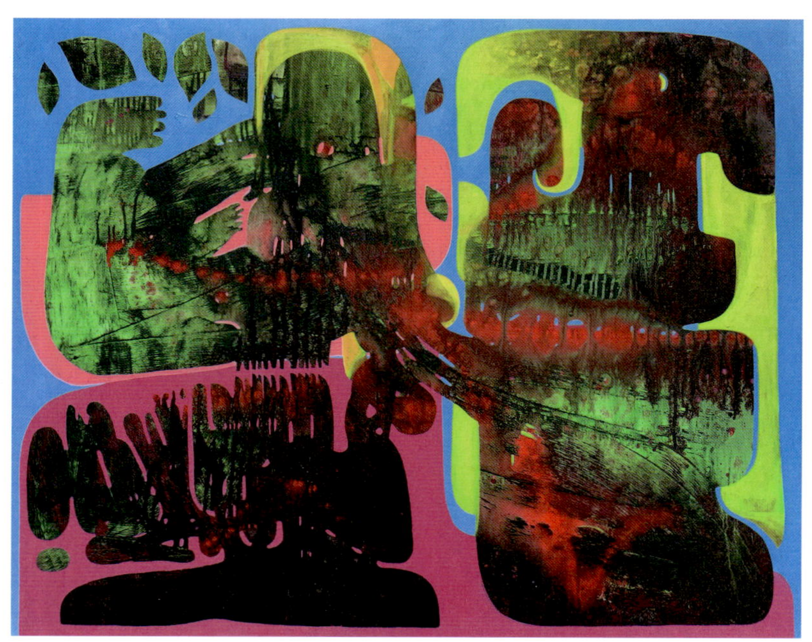

Cherry Pickers, 2022
Oil, acrylic, and pigment on canvas, 48 in. × 60 in. (122 × 152.4 cm)
Museum of Contemporary Art San Diego; Museum purchase with funds from Henry Heuser, 2024.24

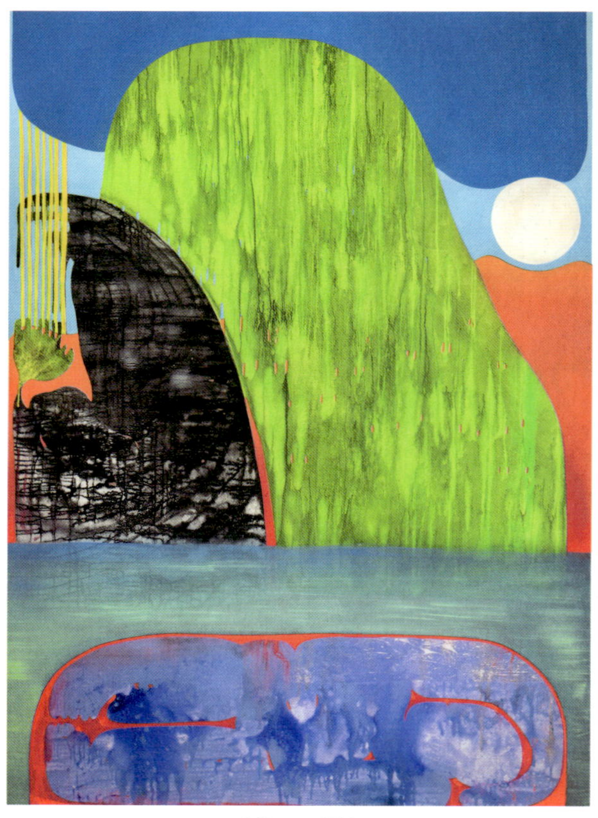

Dilmun, 2022
Oil, acrylic, and pigment on canvas, 80 in. × 60 in. (203.2 cm × 154.2 cm)
Santa Barbara Museum of Art, Museum purchase with funds provided by the General Art Acquisition Fund

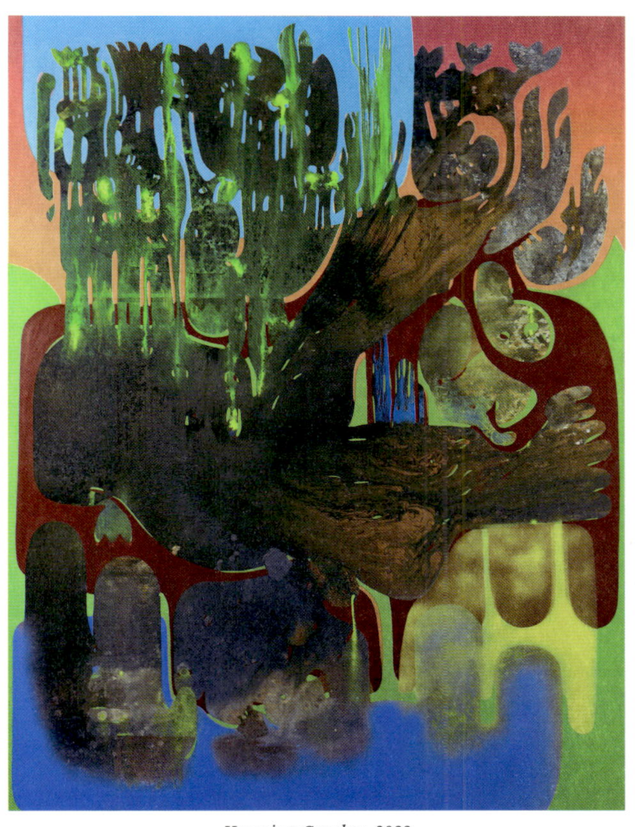

Hanging Garden, 2022
Oil, acrylic, and pigment on canvas, 70 in. × 55 in.
(177.8 cm × 139.7 cm)

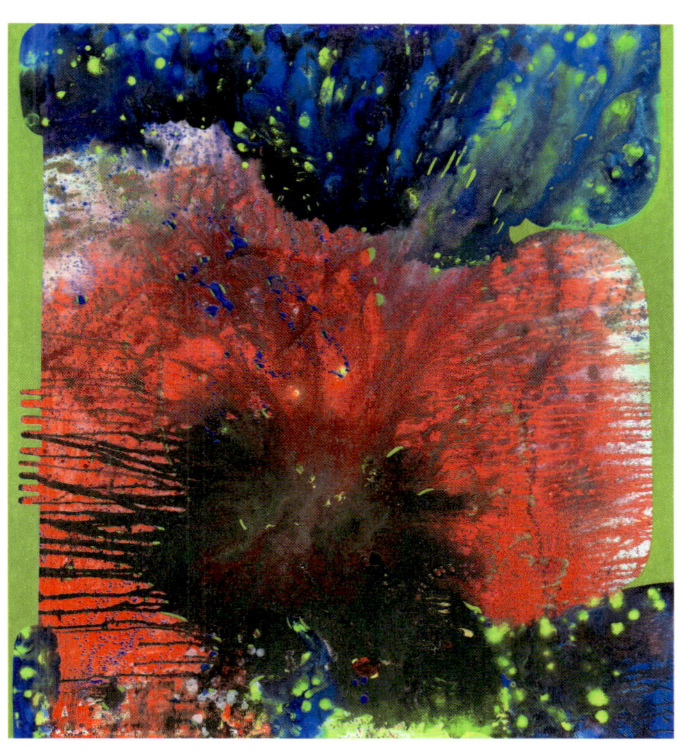

Ecotone I, 2023
Oil, acrylic, and pigment on canvas, 72 in. × 67 in. (183 cm × 170.2 cm)
Shah Garg Collection

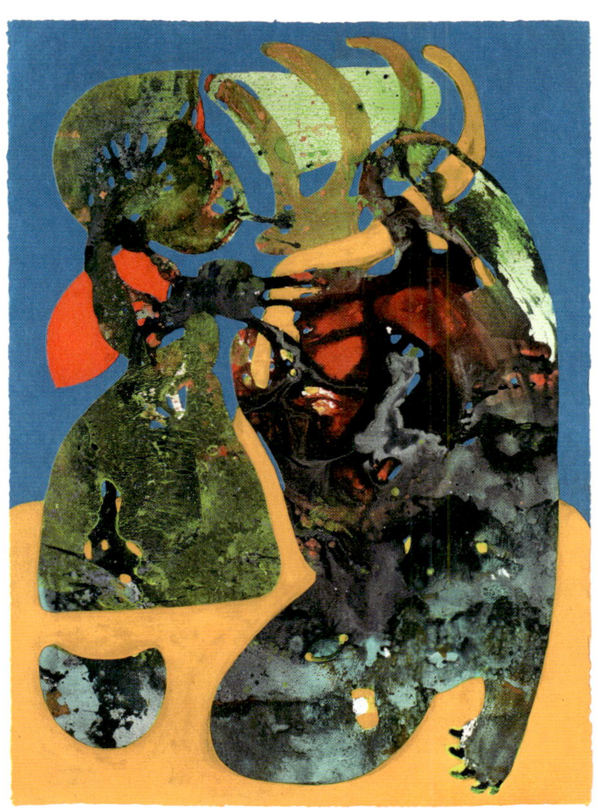

Forest Remains I, 2023
Oil, acrylic, and pigment on Arches paper, 30 in. × 22 ½ in. (76.2 cm × 57.2 cm)
Santa Barbara Museum of Art, Museum purchase
with funds provided by The Basil Alkazzi Acquisition Fund

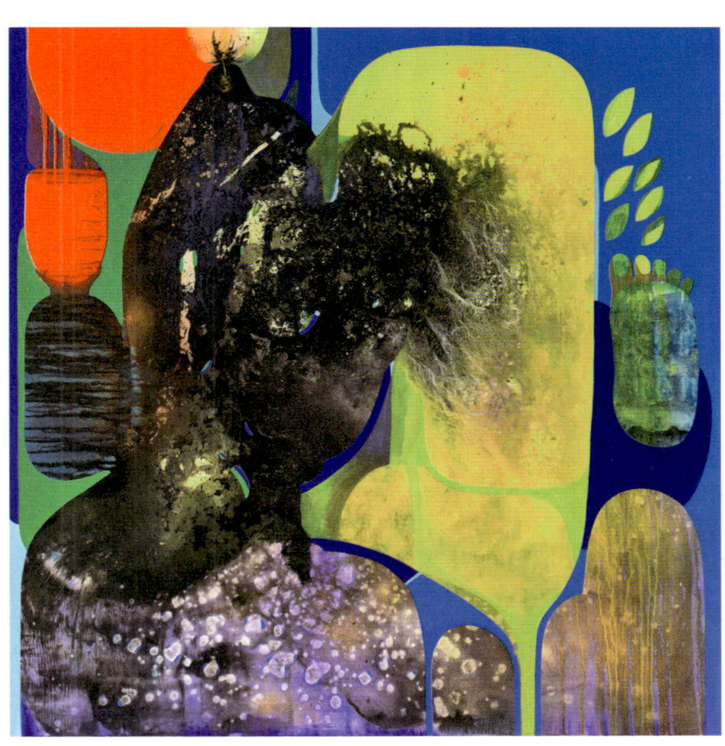

Sanctum, 2023
Oil, acrylic, and pigment on canvas, 62 in. × 62 in. (157.5 cm × 157.5 cm)
Collection of Woo Speed McNaughton

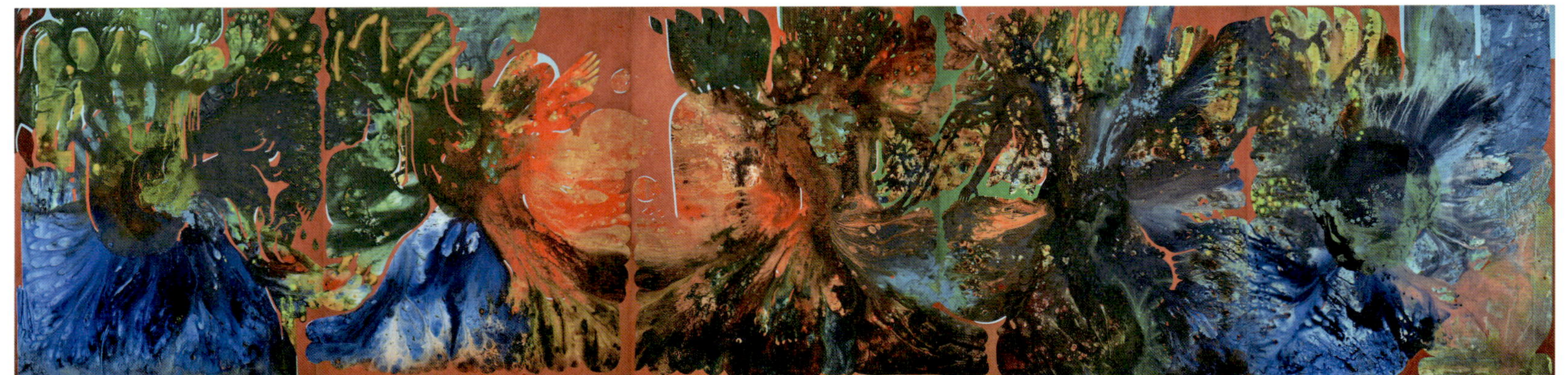

Abzu, 2023
Oil, acrylic, and pigment on canvas, 84 ft. × 29 ft., 6 in. (2.13 m × 8.89 m)

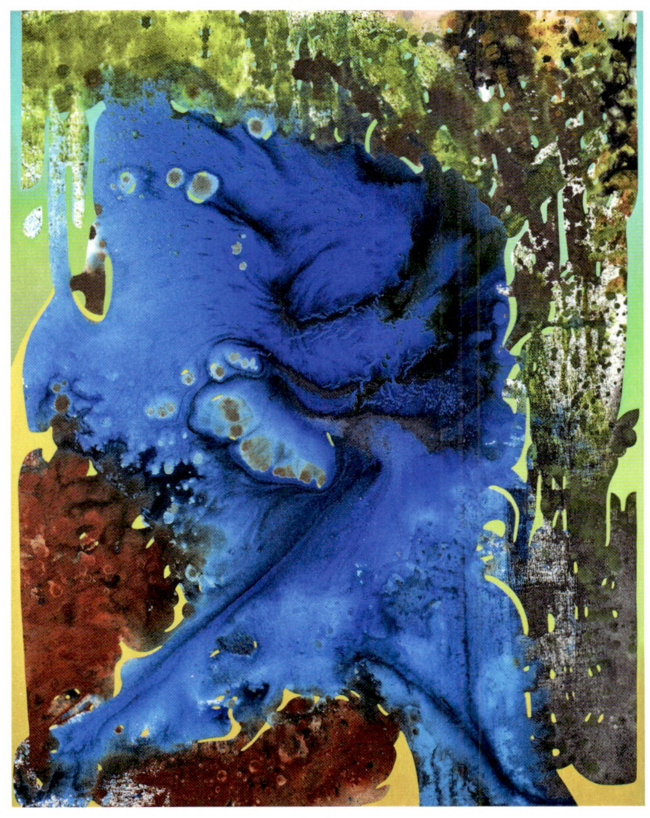

Exhale, 2024
Oil, acrylic, and pigment on canvas, 60 in. × 48 in. (154.2 cm × 122 cm)

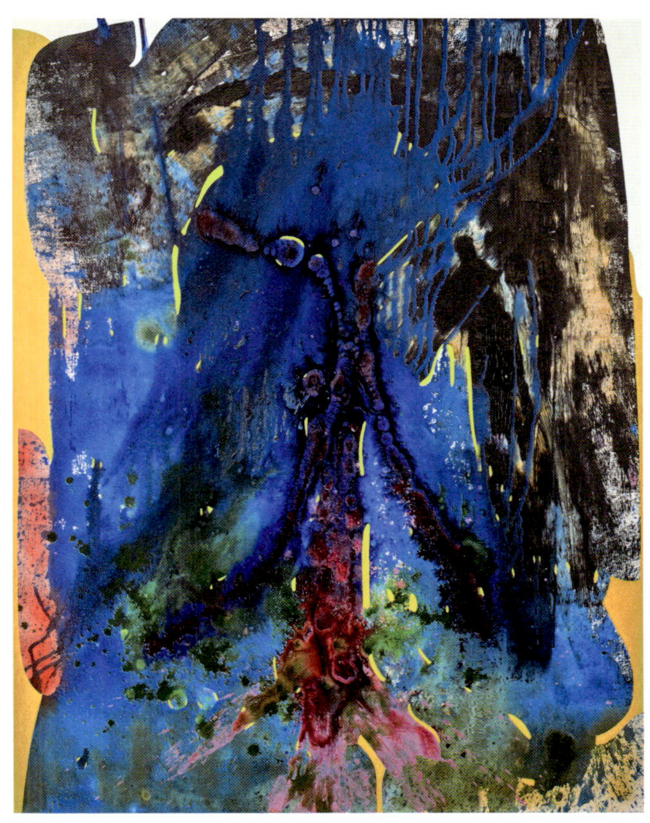

Inhale, 2024
Oil, acrylic, and pigment on canvas, 60 in. × 48 in. (154.2 cm × 122 cm)

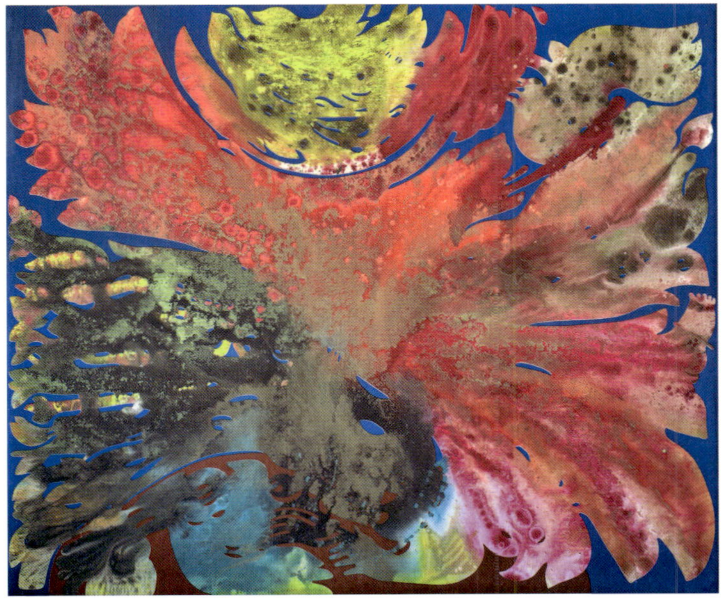

The Sky from Below, 2024–25
Oil, acrylic, and pigment on canvas, 75 in. × 90 in. (190.5 cm × 228.6 cm)

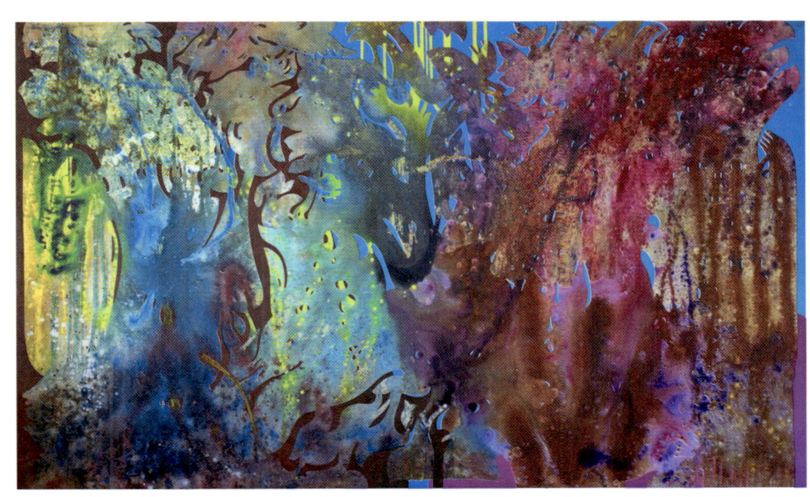

Dual Realms, 2024–25
Oil, acrylic, and pigment on canvas, 91 in. × 150 in. (231.1 cm × 381 cm)

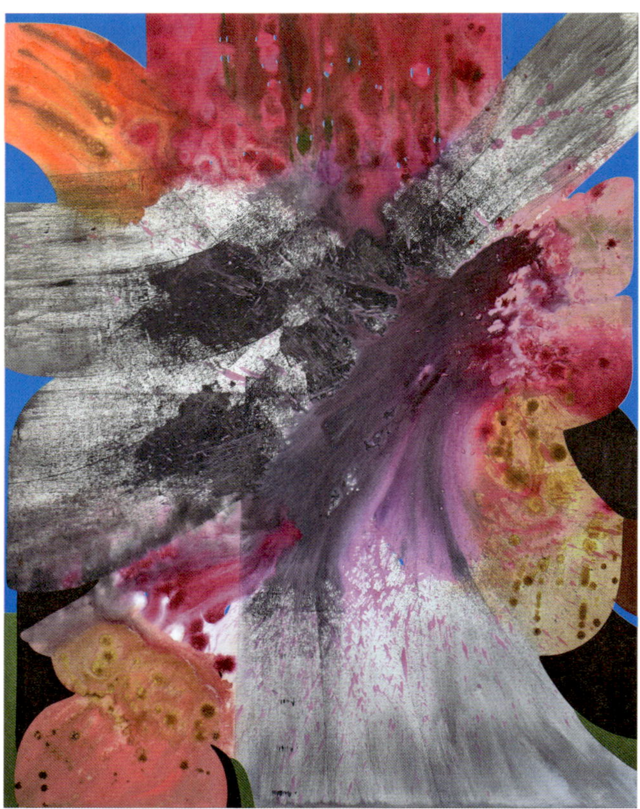

Umm Al-Binni, 2025
Oil, acrylic, and pigment on canvas, 60 in. × 48 in. (154.2 cm × 122 cm)
Private collection, Louisville

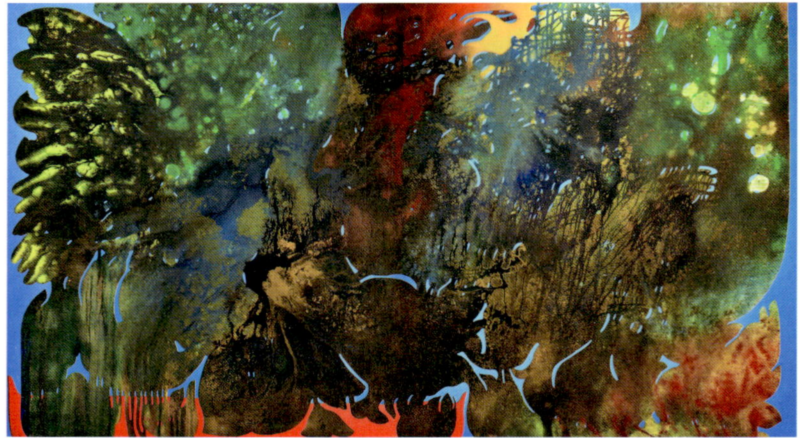

Olivine, 2024
Oil, acrylic, and pigment on canvas, 60 in. × 120 in. (154.2 cm × 304.8 cm)

Vian Sora
Born 1976 in Baghdad, Iraq
Lives and works in Louisville, Kentucky

EDUCATION

2012 MBA, Bellarmine University, Louisville, Kentucky
2007 Printmaking, Istanbul Museum of Graphic Art (IMOGA), Istanbul, Turkey
2000 BS, Al-Mansour University, Baghdad, Iraq

SELECTED SOLO EXHIBITIONS

2025 *Vian Sora: Outerworlds*, Santa Barbara Museum of Art, Santa Barbara, CA; Speed Art Museum, Louisville, KY; Asia Society Texas, Houston, TX

Sky from Below, David Nolan Gallery, New York, NY

2024 *House of Pearls*, The Third Line Gallery, Dubai, UAE
2023 *End of Hostilitie*s, David Nolan Gallery, New York, NY
2022 *Subduction*, Luis De Jesus Los Angeles, Los Angeles, CA

What You Shout into The Woods Echoes Back, Moremen Gallery, Louisville, KY

2021 *Floodgates*, Moremen Gallery, Louisville, KY
2019 *Unbounded Domains*, Moremen Gallery, Louisville, KY
2017 *Now Here*, Quappi Projects, Louisville, KY
2016 *Displaced Narratives*, 1619 Flux, Louisville, KY
2015 *Sacred Journeys*, Festival of Faiths, Actors Theater Gallery, Louisville, KY
2011 *Escape into Life*, US Chamber of Commerce, Washington, D.C.
2010 *Between Two World*s, The Green Building Gallery, Louisville, KY
2007 *Legends of Baghda*d, Showcase Art Gallery, Dubai, UAE

Reflections: Istanbul to Baghdad, IMOGA Art Gallery and Museum of Graphic Art, Istanbul, Turkey

2006 *Voyage into Arabia*, Aspen Gallery, Dar el Cid Museum, Kuwait City, Kuwait

Vian Sora: A Woman in Time, Iraq Museum International Exhibition, Boston, MA

2004 *Longing to Past*, Gallery Zamwa—Sulaymaniyah City, Iraq

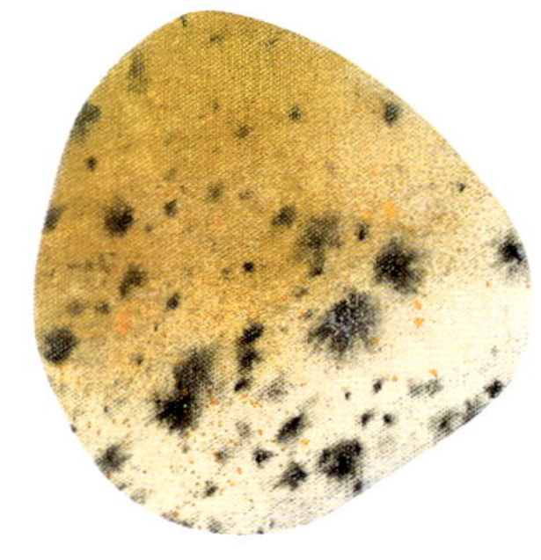

2003 *Vian Sora: Selected Works*, Japanese Foundation Culture Center, Ankara, Turkey

2002 *Neher, Sheher ... Misafirat (River, City...Voyage)*, Topkapi Palace Museum, Istanbul, Turkey

Periphrasis, Baghdad, Grundfos Office Gallery, Baghdad, Iraq

2001 *Pulses, Shapes and Sense of Time*, Inaa Art Gallery, Baghdad, Iraq

SELECTED GROUP EXHIBITIONS

2024 *In the Making: Contemporary Art at SBMA*, Santa Barbara Museum of Art, Santa Barbara, CA

Exposure Therapy, KMAC Contemporary Art Museum, Louisville, KY

Risky Business: A Painter's Forum, Torrance Art Museum, Torrance, CA

2023 *Crosscurrents: Contemporary Art from the Speed Art Museum Collection and Beyond*, Speed Art Museum, Louisville, KY

Rounding the Circle: The Mary and Alfred Shands Collection, Speed Art Museum, Louisville, KY

2022 *Breaking Water*, Contemporary Arts Center, Cincinnati, OH

2021 *New Directions: The Shands Collection*, Quappi Projects, Louisville, KY

2020 *We All Declare For LIBERTY*, Quappi Projects, Louisville, KY

2019 *KMAC TRIENNIAL*, KMAC Contemporary Art Museum, Louisville, KY

Imagined Monuments, Louisville Metro Hall, Louisville, KY

2017 *Project 19: The Prolonged Gaze*, Zephyr Gallery, Louisville, KY

2011 *In the Course of Human Events 9/11–2011*, Louisville Visual Art Association, KY

2010 *Women Imagining Women*, Pyro Gallery, Louisville, KY

2009 *Spring Show*, Total Arts Gallery at the Courtyard, Dubai, UAE

2008 *Selected works by four artists*, Aspen Gallery, Kuwait City, Kuwait

Istanbul Graphic artist annual exhibition, Istanbul Museum of Graphic Art (IMOGA), Istanbul, Turkey

2007 *One Stroke*, Lahd Art Gallery, Riyadh, Saudi Arabia

2006 *East West Dialogues*, Mysticism, Tugra Gallery, London, UK
2005 *Art from the Islamic World*, Aya Gallery, London, UK

Women through War, Al Wasity Art Ministry of Culture Gallery, Baghdad, Iraq

2004 *Autumn Exhibition*, Gallery M, Paris, France
2002 *Four Artist Group Show*, Zamaan Art Gallery, Beirut, Lebanon

Baghdad Art, International Art Festival, Baghdad, Iraq

SPECIAL PROJECTS

2018 *Video Installation*, Collaboration with the Louisville Orchestra, conductor Teddy Abrams, and composer Sebastian Chang, Louisville, KY

AWARDS AND RESIDENCES

2025 Fellowship, Civitella Ranieri Foundation, Visual Arts Residency, Umbria, Italy
2021 Great Meadows Foundation Art Residency Studio Program, Berlin, Germany
2003 Grundfos Art Residency Program August, Bodrum, Turkey
2002 Grundfos Selected Portfolio Artist, Istanbul, Turkey

Grundfos Sponsored Artist, Copenhagen, Denmark

PUBLIC COLLECTIONS

AK Bank Collection, Istanbul, Turkey
Baltimore Museum of Art, Baltimore, MD
Dar Al Cid Museum, Kuwait City
Kuwait French Embassy, Baghdad, Iraq
Fidelity Art Collection, Boston, MA
French Embassy, Baghdad, Iraq
Grinnell College Museum of Art, Grinnell, IA
Italian Embassy, Baghdad, Iraq
KMAC Contemporary Art Museum, Louisville, KY
Ministry of Culture Collection, Baghdad, Iraq
Museum of Contemporary Art San Diego, CA
Pizzuti Collection, Columbus, OH
Santa Barbara Museum of Art, CA
Shah Garg Foundation, New York, NY
Speed Art Museum, Louisville, KY

LENDERS

Erik Eaker
Judson and Daphne Hartlage
Kentucky Performing Arts Foundation
Woo Speed McNaughton
Lopa and Rishabh Mehrotra
Stephanie and Michael Morris
Museum of Contemporary Art San Diego
Santa Barbara Museum of Art
Komal Shah and Gaurav Garg
Brook and Pam Smith
Vian Sora
Speed Art Museum
Drs. Kaveh and Heather Zamanian
A private collection

Major exhibition support is provided by the Great Meadows Foundation.

Support for *Vian Sora: Outerworlds* at the Santa Barbara Museum of Art is provided by SBMA Ambassadors, Joan Davidson, Jeanne Dentzel, Rachel Kaganoff, Isabel and Paul Wendt, and an anonymous donor.

At the time of printing, lead support for *Vian Sora: Outerworlds* at the Speed Art Museum is provided by Brooke and Matthew Barzun and Lopa and Rishabh Mehrotra.

Exhibitions and their related programs at Asia Society Texas are presented by Nancy C. Allen, Chinhui Juhn and Eddie Allen, and Leslie and Brad Bucher. Major support comes from the Brown Foundation, Inc., the City of Houston through Houston Arts Alliance, Houston Endowment Inc. Generous funding also provided by the Anchorage Foundation of Texas, National Endowment for the Arts, and Texas Commission on the Arts. Additional support is provided by the Clayton Fund, Leigh and Reginald Smith, the Stolbun Family, Ann Wales, Judy and Scott Nyquist, the Wortham Foundation, and through contributions from the Exhibitions Patron Circle, a dedicated group of individuals and organizations committed to bringing exceptional visual art to Asia Society Texas.

A decade ago, an unexpected hysterectomy altered my life and while it concluded a biological chapter, it may very well be the impetus for *Outerworlds*, unveiling a connected and shape-shifted consciousness. I woke up completely changed, as did my paintings—transforming the moments of loss, confusion, and pain into a new kind of clarity and creativity. And though it does not yet seem real, this survey is the pinnacle of a career for which I am more than humbled and grateful for all of those who have made this possible. These are the moments when words do not have the ability to transmit our true feelings.

I would be remiss to not first acknowledge the enormous efforts of my grandparents, who transformed a war zone, Baghdad, into a palimpsest with serene gardens nurtured with love, and to my father and mother, who then tended that garden and planted possibility, guidance, and hope within a childhood filled with suffering; you protected me. Their unwavering support of my career is the reason that I am here today. To my husband, thank you.

This exhibition would not be possible without the collective energies of James Glisson, Tyler Blackwell and Owen Duffy, three curatorial visionaries of our time. I am blessed to have this triad of wisdom curate *Outerworlds* and in many ways, back to the origin of the word to "cure;" they have alleviated my anxiety and trepidations during this journey. Thank you Max Harvey and Pianpian He, as your book design and insights made this beautiful object possible. I am honored to have the brilliant Suzanne Hudson contribute her time and words; our conversations are cherished. And to all of the staff at the Santa Barbara Museum of Art, Asia Society Texas, and the Speed Art Museum, thank you dearly; we are one ecosystem where, without you, artists have no air to breathe.

I must acknowledge there is no way to thank all of those who have assisted me throughout my career. In Baghdad, thank you Ghiath Al-Jazairy and Hassan Al-Dahaan from Inaa Art Gallery for your belief in me as well as my friend and then mentor Serwan Baran, and the late, esteemed Noori Al-Rawi. To each of my friends and colleagues from the Associated Press Baghdad office—your protection, courage, and devotion inspired and shaped my works from those harrowing moments.

To the late, wonderful, insightful Reverend Al Shands, who established the Great Meadows Foundation to nurture artists. In our short time, your presence eased my tensions and our moments are treasured. Thank you to Julien Robson for all of you have done.

To Sunny Rahbar and the wonderful team at The Third Line Dubai for the opportunities and understanding of what we must face. To Dr. Omar Kholeif, our moments together are special, and my mind is provoked when we interact; thank you for the forums and conversations. Thank you to Stefania Bortolami and Evan Reiser for your support of my work and especially to Wendy Wahlert at Bortolami for all of your assistance to make this publication happen. And thank you to Luis De Jesus Los Angeles.

I especially want to thank Henry Heuser, Jr. and Donald Whitfield for your early appreciation of my paintings and supporting my career. To Said Baalbaki, I am grateful for your help and support in Berlin. To David Nolan, thank you for trusting in my work. To my dear friend Steve Lindsey for your diligence and willingness to sacrifice that led to an elevated aesthetic environment and creative atmosphere within my studio, a painter's dream.

To all the departed friends and family members whose spirits guided and inspired my artistic journey, I am forever grateful for your unyielding strength and love that permeates within every pore of my creative soul while illuminating a path in the darkest times.

Finally, to all those who have collected my work, loaned paintings, and supported this exhibition, without you none of this is possible. I thank you dearly.

Published on the occasion of the exhibition *Vian Sora: Outerworlds*, organized by:

Tyler Blackwell
Curator of Contemporary Art, Speed Art Museum

Owen Duffy
Nancy C. Allen Curator and Director of Exhibitions, Asia Society Texas

James Glisson
Chief Curator and Curator of Contemporary Art, Santa Barbara Museum of Art

Exhibition Itinerary
Santa Barbara Museum of Art, California
June 15 – September 7, 2025

Speed Art Museum, Louisville, Kentucky
October 10, 2025 – January 18, 2026

Asia Society Texas, Houston, Texas
April 15 – August 2, 2026

Curators
Tyler Blackwell, Owen Duffy, James Glisson

Editors
Owen Duffy and Tyler Blackwell

Copyeditor
Eugenia Bell

Color Management
Yin He, Yi Fan

Printing Coordination
Artron, Shanghai

Publication Coordinator
Zoe Kauder Nalebuff

Publication Design
Studio Pianpian He and Max Harvey

Photography
Lance Brewer (Courtesy of David Nolan Gallery), Chad Crews (Courtesy of Luis de Jesus Gallery), Bob Hower, Altamash Urooj (Courtesy of The Third Line)

Published in 2026 by Inventory Press, Speed Art Museum, and Asia Society Texas

Inventory Press
2305 Hyperion Ave.
Los Angeles, CA 90027
inventorypress.com

Speed Art Museum
2035 South Third Street
Louisville, KY 40208
speedmuseum.org

Asia Society Texas
1370 Southmore Blvd.
Houston, TX 77004
asiasociety.org/texas

ISBN: 978-1-941753-84-2
LCCN: 2025942859

Distributed by
ARTBOOK | D.A.P.
75 Broad St, Suite 630
New York, NY 10004
artbook.com

Printed and bound in China

www.inventorypress.com

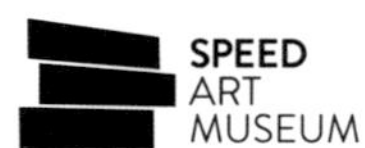

Front cover: Vian Sora, *Floodgates*, 2021. Oil, acrylic, and pigment on canvas, 72 × 96 in. Courtesy of Kentucky Performing Arts Foundation. Photo by Bob Hower.

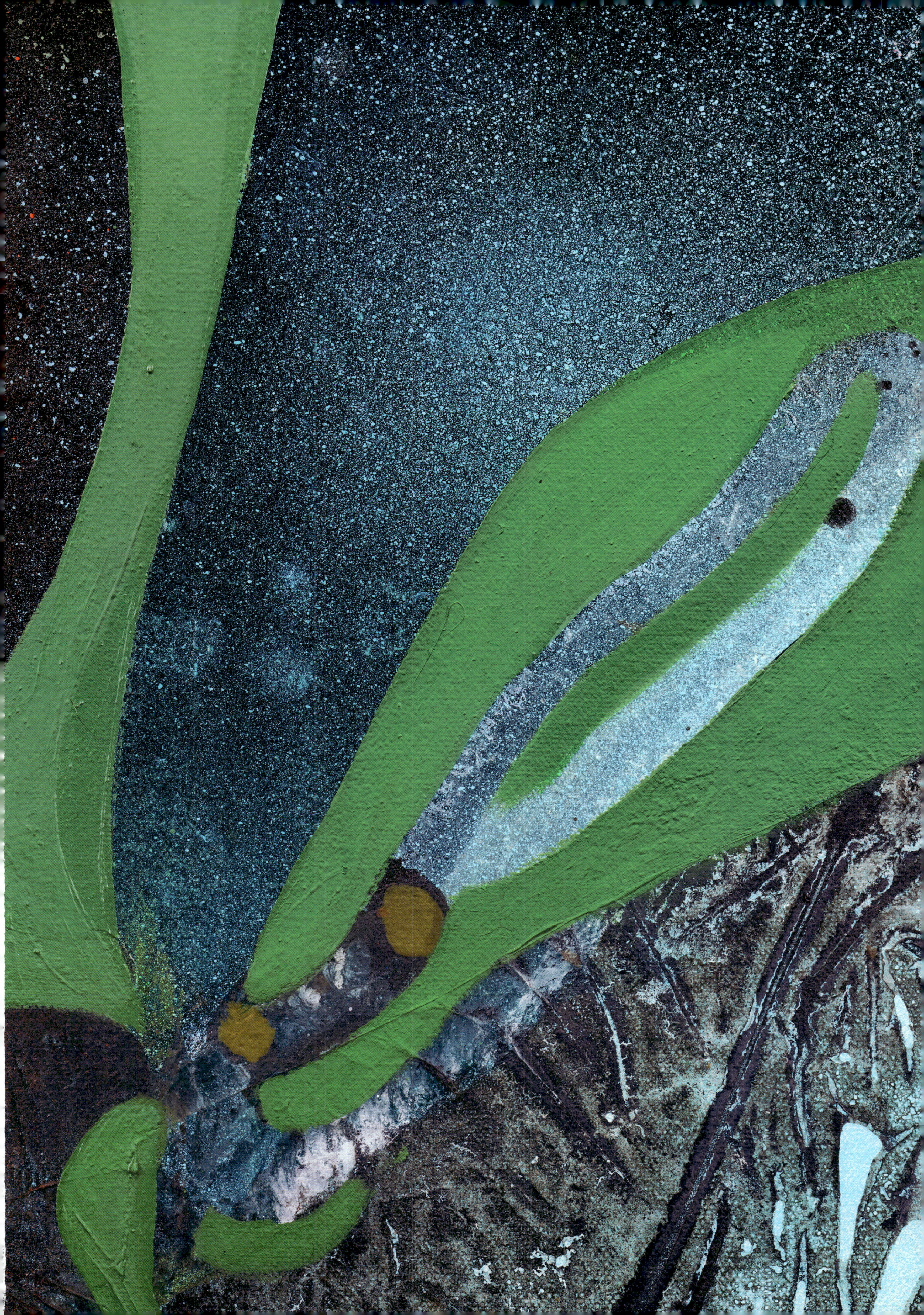

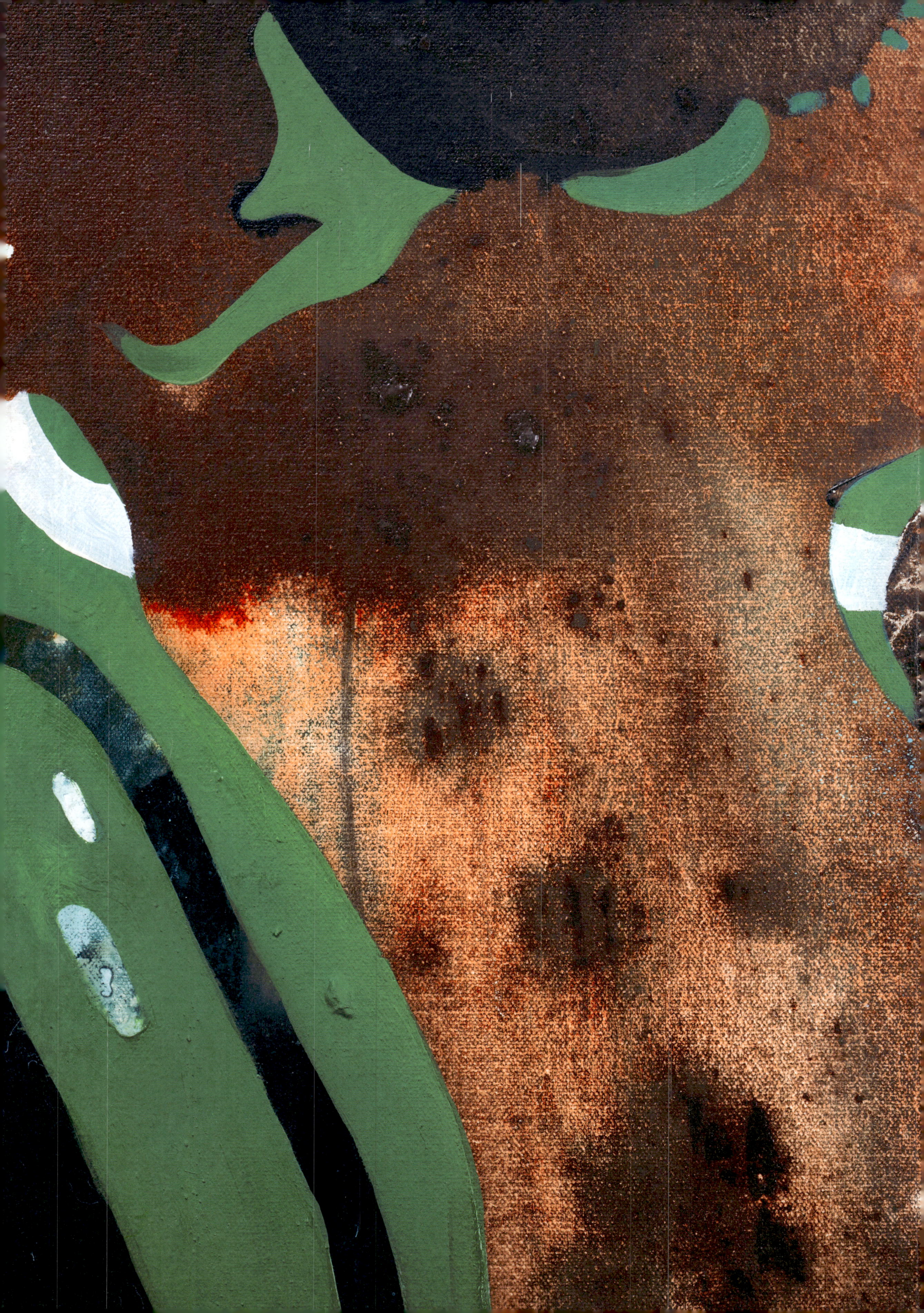